The Amazons

MERINA VALASCA

Astrolog Publishing House

Cover Design: Na'ama Yaffe
Layout and Graphics: Daniel Akerman
Production Manager: Dan Gold

P.O. Box 1123, Hod Hasharon 45111, Israel
Tel: 972-9-7412044
Fax: 972-97442714

ISBN 965-494-199-6

Published by Astrolog Publishing House 2005

Highlights...

MUNIFICENTIA·SS·D·N·BENEDICTI·PP·XIV·A·D·MDCCX

The Amazons

The word Amazon appears in virtually every modern language and conjures many meanings and provocative images. Webster's dictionary calls an Amazon a "tall manly woman", but most people think of Amazons as "fighters" or "warriors" as well. At times the label Amazon is given derogatorily to a woman who is perceived as too aggressive or physically imposing. Women with special prowess in horsemanship or marksmanship are also sometimes called Amazons. Modern males have a love-hate relationship with the idea of a warrior woman. While on the one hand such overly aggressive women are certainly a threatening element, many find them magnetically attractive. A popular television series featuring just such a woman fighter attests to the fascination (perhaps among both sexes) the subject and its images engender.

In general, the modern consensus holds that the original Amazons were a race or tribe of warrior women who existed either in reality or in fantasy, during ancient times. Mythically or actually, the Amazon nation constituted a contradiction to virtually every society before or since – a nation not only ruled and dominated by women, but where women were the only viable citizens. Theirs was a society based on all of the values normally considered 'non-womanly' by almost every culture known to Earth.

Who were the Amazons? Did they actually exist, living and fighting over a period of hundreds, perhaps thousands of years? Where and how are they said to have lived, and how did they affect the surrounding contemporary and future cultures? Were they perhaps the fruit of overactive male Greek imaginations? Or did such tribes actually exist whose stories have been embellished and preserved until they took on mythical proportions? Most of our knowledge of the Amazons comes down from the Greek myths and historical writings and from works of art in various media which have been preserved from ancient times. There is even a theory that the Centaurs (creatures with four legs of the horse and human torsos and heads) of Greek myth were actually depictions of Amazon women on horseback. Records of tribes of female warriors have come down in Hittite, Indian, Scythian and Chinese writings as well.

Recent archeological discoveries have convinced many researchers that much of what is told in the myths and depicted in ancient art indeed had a basis in reality. In what is now Russia, female skeletons have been unearthed with weapons at their sides. The leg muscles of a teenage girl were bowed in such as way as to suggest that her formative years had been

spent on horseback. Another young woman was found with an arrowhead embedded in her body, pointing to death in battle. Skeletons of younger children were also found, but always near adult males. In areas somewhat outside the traditional boundaries of what is thought to be Amazon territory, remains of female warriors have been discovered, buried along with weapons and even horses. While not enough has been uncovered to "prove" all of the stories handed down by the ancient scribes, it is difficult to dismiss the very real possibility that the Amazons were real.

The picture that emerges is an interesting and colorful one, complete with contradictions and numerous possible interpretations, making it all the more fascinating. A nation of women only, whose culture was based on the acquisition and use of equestrian and fighting skills, the Amazons were women of war. In fact or in fantasy they clashed with various male enemies over a vast geographical area and a long span of years.

There is no real consensus as to the origin of the term Amazon, although several plausible theories exist. In the ancient Persian language, the phrase "uma soona" meant "moon children". In Armenian a similar phrase meant "Moon woman" or "moon warrior". Since the Amazons are sometimes depicted carrying moon-shaped shields and were said to have worshipped Artemis, the goddess of the moon, it is thought that these may explain the name. Other researchers have concluded that the word Amazon corresponds to a Greek phrase "a – mazos", or "amazoi" meaning "breast less".

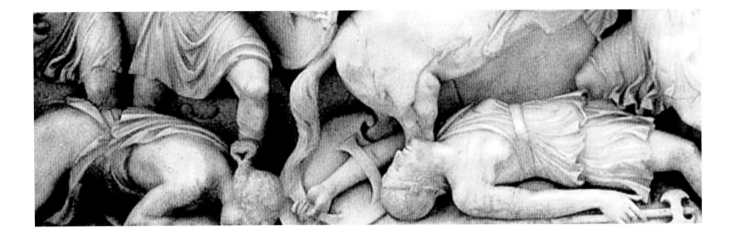

The Amazons of Greek Myth and History

Historical and mythological accounts provided by quite a number of writers have been preserved. Homer gave us fascinating stories of the Amazons in the Iliad. Indeed, his are the earliest accounts, written around 750 BC. Strabo, Diodorus, and Pliny are but a few more of authors who told of the warrior women from the vantage point of history, writing several hundred years after their stories were to have taken place. The great historians Plutarch and Herodotus disagreed as to the truth or fiction of the Amazon nation. Plutarch maintained that the Amazons were purely mythical, while Herodotus, who called them "man-killers" believed in the actual existence of such "warrior women" (perhaps not in a female warrior "nation" however). What follows is a brief synthesis of what is "known" about the Amazons and their way of life.

Most Greek accounts place the beginnings of the Amazon nation somewhere in the second or third centuries B.C., although some have placed them even earlier. Some artistic renderings of what could be Amazons date back to the eight century BC. Of the exact locations in which the Amazons lived and fought, we may never be certain. It is generally agreed that their capital city was Themiscrya, in Pontus, on the banks of the River Thermodon, which flowed into the Euxinus Sea (known today as the Black Sea, in what is now Turkey). Many writers place the Amazons in the Caucasus Mountain Range, all the way to the Caspian Sea. The first queen to rule the Amazon nation in this area was Lysippe, who established the city of Themyscira in the area which is today Terme, Turkey. They are said also to have established numerous other cities, including Ephesus, on the west coast of Asia Minor (a peninsula of land with coasts on the Black Sea to the north, the Aegean Sea to the west, and the Mediterranean to the south). Other Amazon cities were Sinope, Paphos, and Smyrna. From their Thermodon base, the Amazons made war against the people of Scythia, Asia Minor, the islands of the Aegean Sea, and perhaps even lands as far-flung as Syria and Egypt and even India. They were based mainly in the mountains the plains next to the Caspian Sea, between the Albanians and the Iberians, were also Amazon country. They preferred mountainous terrain and the seclusion of wooded areas, as well as the isolation of islands.

Paphos

There are several accounts as to where and how the Amazon culture originally came into being. According to one story, the Scythian people had a gripe against two members of their royalty, Hylinos and Scoloptos, whom they eventually banished along with large entourages of family members, slaves, and other followers. These princes marched their citizens to the Causasus and up the foothills. As they cut a swathe through the countryside, the Scythian men plundered and stole, making themselves generally hated, until the wronged indigenous peoples decided to fight back. They succeeded in wiping out nearly the entire male population of the followers of the two princes, leaving a "nation" of displaced females and their children. The women were grief stricken and extremely angry at the murder of their husbands, sons, brothers, and fathers, and turned their considerable rage against their neighbors and then against men in general. Refusing to be absorbed into the communities of the murdering enemies, the women set up their own state in the mountains.

The women had to become tough to defend their autonomous position and indeed spent a large amount of time and energy fending off enemies who would have happily done away with the strange female state. Fighting with their neighbors soon took a toll on the population, and in due time they found it necessary to replenish their numbers. Obviously males would be needed in order to provide for the continuation of the group. The most plausible theory as to how the Amazons solved this involves truces with neighboring male armies, and fornication with the "enemy". They may have had a yearly agreement with the neighboring Gargareans which entailed meeting for sexual relations aimed at providing the Amazons with offspring. Prisoners of war were often pressed into service for this purpose as well, provided they were deemed suitable specimens. Female infants of such unions were kept within the tribe and raised by their mothers. Conflicting theories abound as to what became of the male infants. They may have been returned to their fathers, or simply put to death at birth. There are some accounts, however, that the males were brought up in the Amazon society and later used for procreation. Others say the boys were mutilated by castration or that their limbs were dislocated, and that these injured males were kept as domestics who served the female warriors. Rendering them lame from the outset assured the women that the men could not organize and rise up against them later. Some stories even suggest that the Amazon women consumed the flesh of their male infants. Others point to the use of male infants as sacrifices to the gods.

The girl children were brought up harshly and trained to a life of fighting. Rather than mother's milk, the children were fed the milk of mares, and were introduced early to solid foods.

The story has been passed down that the right breast of infant girls (some say the left breast) would be seared at birth, so as to assure the flatness of the chest on that side, supposedly allowing more efficient use of the bow and spear. Other accounts say the breast was removed when it began to develop. Interestingly, however, as prevalent as this belief is, none of the depictions of the Amazons in ancient art back it up. Amazons are always shown with two intact breasts or with draped clothing over the right breast. The belief may have resulted from the theory that the name came from the Greek "breast less", rather than the other way around. Perhaps "breast less" was simply a euphemism for "masculine", rather than a direct reference to the removal of breasts. It has been noted as well, that many women have achieved champion status as archers with both breasts firmly in place!

The structure of Amazon society has not been described in detail, but most accounts agree that they appointed two queens that ruled simultaneously. One queen's domain was domestic affairs, including agriculture, husbandry, and other economical concerns, while the other queen led the military and ruled over all that concerned war and relations with other groups.

The Amazon lifestyle was extremely demanding. The raising of horses fit for use in battle was a major occupation, alongside agricultural activities necessary for nourishment of the tribes. Some writers have described the Amazons as tamers of wild beasts (such as lions, deer, and falcons) as well as keepers of domestic animals. Hunting, both on foot and on horseback, was also one of the Amazons' main pursuits, and the skills needed for war were in some ways parallel to those needed for the hunt.

While there is some debate as to whether males constituted part of the Amazon society in some capacity or other, there is no doubt that arms were born by females only. The Amazons were not "hearth and home" types. They did not make war simply to defend their lands. Rather, they were an aggressive and zealous war-making machine, greatly feared by their neighboring tribes. The

Amazons were ruthless warriors, showing no mercy to their enemies and no reticence whatever in battle. Ancient Greek soldiers have been described as suffering trauma and "withered manhood" at the mere thought of an Amazon attack.

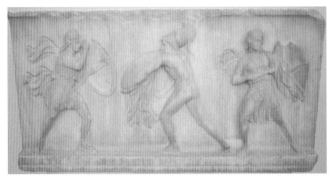

The Amazon girl was required to remain a virgin for the duration of her service as a warrior. When her prime had been spent on defending the tribe, she could turn her attention to procreation, and perhaps, motherhood, although some accounts say that males were actually employed as "nannies" for the girl children until they were given over to military training.

Girls began their equestrian training early, and learned to wield their weapons agilely while astride a steed. The Amazon warriors were accomplished foot-soldiers as well. Their weaponry included the bow and arrow, several types of javelins and spears, and a special double-edged battle axe, inspired by the mighty Hittites, which struck particular fear in the hearts of their adversaries. They carried shields shaped as crescent moons, or smallish round shields.

Whether they had one breast or two, the Amazon women excelled in the use of the weapons of the times. They were skilled markswomen with both the bow and the spear. Many authors have

waxed in awe about the Amazon skill at archery, the tremendous speed of their arrows, and their devastatingly accurate aim. The Amazons were also outstanding equestrians, brilliantly using the strength and speed of horses as excellent compensation for their natural disadvantages in size, height and brawn against their male enemies. It is thought by some that the Amazons were actually the first humans to ride on horseback, or at the very least, the first to ride horses into military battle. It is possible that the Greeks took the idea of using cavalry from the Amazons. The stirrup was said to have been invented by the Amazons, as well as the spur. The horses were not heavily girded or armored, making them light on their feet and maneuverable. Speed was of the essence, as was strategy.

Making war was the Amazon claim to fame. Trumpets often announced the advance of Amazon troops and sometimes other instruments as well. Often a barbarous dance was performed to the music as they began their march toward the battle. The Amazons often charged headlong into the enemy's ranks, while simultaneously letting go a barrage of arrows and darts. Then, before the opposing army had time to rally, they turned their horses quickly around and swiftly retreated. Their retreat, however, was often as deadly as their original attack, since the Amazons would rotate on their horses' backs, and continue shooting – backward – as their animals sped away. Another tactic was to rush in and engage the enemy in one on one fighting at close range, where the Amazon on horseback had a clear advantage over her enemy on foot. Some authors have described the use of nets in connection with the Amazons, and these may have been real or figurative. It is possible that nets were thrown over the heads of the enemy, strangling him or rendering him helpless enough to be cut down with a lance. Another theory postulates that the "net" was a euphemism for a feminine "trap" or trickery, and not an actual physical weapon.

Depictions of Amazons in Greek sculpture and painting abound. They were a favorite subject for painters, sculptors, and potters. Ancient art depicting the Amazons usually shows them on horseback and armed for battle, so we have little knowledge as to their "home life" or garb when not at war. In the earliest art the Amazons wore short tunics, with the skirts coming to just above the knees. Usually the fabric was draped over left shoulder, leaving the right breast exposed. Girdles were worn, which cinched the women at the waist, on the outside of the clothing, gathering the fabric of the garment. These tunics may have been made from the skins of animals killed in the hunt, and if so, the leather provided a bit of additional protection against darts flung by the enemy. In later works of art, the tunic became a bit longer and more draped, as if made of lengths of fabric. Leg armor was usually worn from the ankle to the knee, and sometimes spurs were attached to these. Sandals or boots were sometimes worn, but most Amazons seem to have gone barefoot, even on horseback and into battle. Headgear consisted of leather helmets, often decorated with impressive plumes. Flaps covering the ears and neck were common additions to the helmet. After the Amazon's excursions to Persia, their dress began to show aspects of Persian influence. Their tunics became close-fitting sheaths, and they sported hats which resembled those worn by Persians of the time.

The Amazons were considered a race and nation apart from that of Greece, and they had their own fully developed culture. Since "wild" women were anything but the norm in Greek, especially Athenian society, the Amazons, whether in myth or in reality, were no doubt seen as a warning or example of what a woman should not aspire to be. They were admired for their fighting skills, but they were also feared and perhaps even hated.

The Amazons were likely as religiously oriented as the rest of humanity in during the centuries they lived in. They worshipped a fairly vast pantheon of gods, most of which corresponded with those of the Greeks. One theory holds that the Amazons began as a group of priestesses who served at the temple of Artemis and that in this capacity it is possible the searing of the right breast (if it took place at all) constituted priestly self-mutilation, in parallel to the self-castration of male priests. Artemis was worshipped as the goddess of hunting and wild animals, especially bears. Her great shrine was erected at Ephesus. She was the huntress for the Olympian gods, and while she killed animals in the hunt, she was ironically also considered a protector of the wild beasts and of the forests and nature. Artemis was also associated with moon and the lunar cycle, and was considered a champion of women, meting out swift punishment to anyone who would cause them harm. She was the protector of newborns and young children, and as such was a goddess of childbirth. Artemis herself was a sworn virgin however, and her influence stopped at motherhood. She took an oath witnessed by Zeus to remain pure and untouched by male hands. Virginity was thus highly regarded and strictly preserved by Amazon society, given up only out of necessity for procreation. The myth of the nymph Callisto points out the importance of virginity to the goddess Artemis, who demanded that her female attendants uphold the same purity that she did. According to the story, Callisto was impregnated by the god Zeus, which infuriated Artemis who turned her into a she-bear as punishment.

This myth was so ingrained into Greek culture that every year a festival was held commemorating the story of the she-bear. Young girls would disguise themselves as bears during the festival, reenacting the myth as a lesson and rite of passage.

Artemis is depicted in Greek art in the company of dogs and nymphs, and is often driven in a silver chariot pulled by deer. She appears as a tall young girl. She carried a bow, but did not have the countenance of a warrior or a particularly threatening persona.

Some writers contend that the Amazons were descendents of Ares, through his mating with

Harmonia. The Greek god of war, Ares was also seen as the deity of anger and wrath. Ares was thought to be very aggressive and given to fits of rage, and so were the Amazons. Strabo attributed to the Amazons rites of worship which were quite barbarous. He believed they offered human (always male) sacrifices to Ares and then consumed the flesh of the sacrificial man or boy.

Cybele, too, was an important goddess to the Amazons. As the mother of the Olympian gods, Cybele (also known as the Titan goddess Rhea) was a fertility goddess and patroness of motherhood. Cybele was associated closely with the moon, and represented the female monthly cycle as well as the entire womanly life cycle. Under the guidance of Cybele, women were believed to pass through three periods of life. From childhood virginity they passed into motherhood, and ultimately became crones during the final cycle of wisdom and ripe old age.

Greek Heroes and the Amazons

LIBYA

An additional, earlier Amazon society is documented by the historical and mythical literature. It was established in southern and western Libya, its capital city being Cherronesus. This race would have existed hundreds of years before the Amazon society that peopled the Thermodon valley, but cultural characteristics similar to the latter were attributed to this earlier Amazon nation. Diodorus of Sicily wishing to set the historical record straight concerning the Amazons and mankind's persistent belief that the Thermodon race was the one and only, wrote a rather lengthy account of them.

At the time that the Libyan Amazons were living and warring, according to Greek Myth, the lost civilization of Atlantis was supposed to have been thriving. Atlantis was said to be a vast fertile island populated by an advanced and sophisticated society which excelled in all endeavors including farming, trade, and commerce. The great philosopher, Plato believed that Atlantis was a real, rather than mythical place, and his description of the island has many parallels with that of Minoan Crete, which was indeed wiped out by volcanic explosion which took place on the nearby

continent. The volcanic activity might well have caused a huge tidal wave which swallowed up the island, and this may be the source of the belief that Atlantis met its end by sinking into the sea.

The Greeks wove many stories involving the Atlantis which they believed was founded by Poseidon, God of the Sea. From Poseidon sprang a lineage of gods, leading to Atlantis being called the "birthplace of the gods". Atlas was the first king of Atlantis, and subsequent kings were gods of Greek mythology. The story goes that the Atlantians thought of themselves as immortal, which angered Zeus who brought the great flood that wiped them out as punishment.

Diodorus of Sicily placed the Libyan Amazons on the Island of Hespera, off the western coast. This huge island was actually amid a marshland at the point where the River Triton flowed into the ocean. Diodorus described the island as rich in natural resources, a paradise fruit trees were plentiful and where goats, sheep and other small animals were easily hunted for food. The island had several cities, all of which were overtaken by the Amazons with the exception of the sacred city of Mene. They founded their own capital city, called Cherronesus

As we might expect, the Amazons went on the aggressive against neighboring Atlantis. The great Queen of the Amazons, Myrina, raised an army of thirty thousand warrior women. In addition to foot soldiers Myrina commanded three thousand cavalry troops who were trained to a pinnacle of horsemanship and warrior skills. With this formidable battalion she swept into Atlantis and attacked the city of Cerne. After a bloody campaign, Cerne fell and the Amazons took prisoner all the Atlantians who remained alive. In a rare show of cruelty to their opponents, all of the captured Cerne men were put to death, and the women and children taken into slavery.

When the citizens of the other cities of Atlantis got wind of what had happened in Cerne, they gave themselves up to Myrina without conflict, offering her lavish gifts and their willingness to do anything required to make her their friend. Diodorus assures us that Myrina heard their pleas, stopped her attacks on Atlantis, and indeed befriended the rest of their people. Cerne was razed to the ground, and a new city founded on its ruins. The Atlantians heaped honors on Myrina and treated her as a respected ruler.

Here we must mention another tribe of warlike women, the Gorgons, that had been a constant threat and worry to Atlantis. According to Greek myth, the Gorgons were a trio of atrocious female monsters. Their names were Stheno, Euryale, and Medusa, and they were the triplet offspring of Phorkys and Keto, the mythological brother and sister

pair of sea deities whose mating brought many mythical monsters into being. The first two were said to have inherited their parents' immortality, while Medusa was mortal. The monstrous countenance of the Gorgons made them frightening creatures indeed. They had bodies of winged dragons, with human heads topped with writing snakes in place of hair. What made the Gorgons particularly dangerous was their ability to turn any person or beast that fell under their glance into stone.

The Gorgons described by Diodorus in connection with the Amazons and the Atlantians, however, did not seem to be mythical monsters and they were certainly considerably more than three in number! These Gorgons seemed almost similar to the Amazons in that they were a race of human female warriors. These Gorgons were a constant threat and nuisance to Atlantis, and after the Amazons took power there the Atlantians beseeched Myrina to use her powerful war skills to rout the Gorgons once and for all.

Myrina agreed, and soon the Amazons marched against the Gorgons where they were met with heavy resistance from the other female force. A particularly pitched battle ensued at the end of which the Amazons managed to prevail, but after heavy losses were suffered on both sides. Numerous Gorgons fell into Amazon captivity, but others tried to escape, seeking cover in a nearby wooded area. Myrina was determined to trap them and ordered the forest burned around them. Even this, however, failed to entirely destroy the Gorgons, but the Amazons tired of the effort to wipe them out completely and retreated back to their city, taking more than three thousand Gorgon prisoners in tow.

The Amazons undoubtedly thought that their victory had been decisive enough to warrant some quiet from the Gorgons for quite some time. What happened next no doubt took them by complete surprise. Amazon warriors always slept with their weapons at their sides, and those guarding the Gorgon captives were certainly no exceptions. While they slumbered, the Gorgon prisoners staged an uprising of such suddenness and force that they succeeded in killing many of the Amazon soldiers by grabbing up the weapons of the sleeping women and using them to mercilessly stab them. The Amazons suffered losses, but in due time they rallied, and soon had massacred the Gorgon prisoners, leaving not a single one alive.

(The Gorgons at some point rose to strength again, since according to Greek myth, Medusa later became their queen and clashed with both Perseus and Heracles.)

Myrina ordered an honorable and mass funeral to be held for the fallen Amazons. Three giant funeral pyres were erected atop woman-made hills of earth which were later called the Amazon Mounds.

Myrina led her Amazons in further adventures which purportedly took them throughout the Libyan mainland where they battled all of the indigenous tribes, emerging victorious time and again. They continued their expeditions over a vast area which included most of the then known world. Reaching as far as Egypt, Myrina befriended Horus, the son of the great Egyptian gods Osiris and Isis, who was at that time Pharaoh, and himself considered a god. Myrina's warriors even ventured into Syria, subduing all who dared to oppose them. They continued into Asia Minor, leaving only the Cilicians at peace, since the latter, rather than meet the marauders with resistance, approached the Amazons bearing gifts and declarations of willingness to cede to Myrina's rule. Numerous cities were founded during these expeditions, including Pitana, Priene, and Cyme.

The Amazons of Libya continued along the sea, seizing islands on their way, one of which was the island of Lesbos, where Myrina founded the city of Mitylene after her sister, one of the warriors that took part in the battle there. During these island campaigns, a great storm suddenly caught the Amazons, some of whom who were carried off with Myrina to a deserted island. After dreaming that she must do so, Myrina prayed and offered sacrifices to the goddess Cybele whom Diodorus calls "Mother of the Gods", asking for protection and deliverance. She named their island refuge Samothrace, meaning "sacred island" in Greek.

Assumedly, the prayers were answered and the Amazons returned safely home, since Diodorus goes on to describe an invasion of their land by Thracians. The Amazons tried mightily to hold off the Thracian force, but in the end most of them perished, including Queen Myrina. Those few Amazons that survived retreated quietly and thus ended the era of the Libyan Amazons.

During the twentieth century, in Libya's uninhabited stone dessert, ancient rock engravings were discovered which depicted female fighters eerily similar to those depicted in Greek art dated centuries later. One such carving shows a woman armed with a bow and arrows, wearing the pointed head gear characteristic of the later Amazons.

HERCULES next labour was of a more delicate kind. Admeta, the daughter of Eurystheus, longed to obtain the girdle of the queen of the Amazons, and Eurystheus ordered Hercules to go and get it. The Amazons were a nation of women. They were very warlike and held several flourishing cities. It was their custom to bring up only the female children; the boys were either sent away to the neighbouring nations or put to death. Hercules was accompanied by a number of volunteers, and after various adventures at last reached the country of the Amazons. Hippolyta, the queen, received him kindly, and consented to yield him her girdle, but Juno, taking the form of an Amazon, went and persuaded the rest that the strangers were carrying off their queen. They instantly armed and came in great numbers down to the ship. Hercules, thinking that Hippolyta, had acted treacherously, slew her, and taking her girdle made sail homewards.

BULFINCH'S MYTHOLOGY

Resistless thro' the war Camilla rode,
In danger unappall'd, and pleas'd with blood.
One side was bare for her exerted breast;
One shoulder with her painted quiver press'd.
Now from afar her fatal jav'lins play;
Now with her ax's edge she hews her way:
Diana's arms upon her shoulder sound;
And when, too closely press'd, she quits the ground,
From her bent bow she sends a backward wound.
Her maids, in martial pomp, on either side,
Larina, Tulla, fierce Tarpeia, ride:
Italians all; in peace, their queen's delight;
In war, the bold companions of the fight.
So march'd the Tracian Amazons of old,
When Thermodon with bloody billows roll'd:
Such troops as these in shining arms were seen,
When Theseus met in fight their maiden queen:
Such to the field Penthisilea led,
From the fierce virgin when the Grecians fled;

With such, return'd triumphant from the war,
Her maids with cries attend the lofty car;
They clash with manly force their moony shields;
With female shouts resound the Phrygian fields.

The Aeneid by *Virgil*

Publius Vergilius Maro (70-19 BC)
is considered the finest of all Roman poets.

Hippodamia, who, excited by the brave deeds of Penthesilea and her companions, calls upon the Trojan maids and matrons:

"Come, friends, let us too in our hearts conceive
A martial spirit such as now inflames
Our warriors fighting for their native walls;
For not in strength are we inferior much
To men; the same our eyes, our limbs the same;
One common light we see, one air we breathe;
Nor different is the food we eat. What then
Denied to us hath Heaven on man bestowed?
O let us hasten to the glorious war!"

Quintus Smyrnus

Achilles killing Penthesilea

The Subjection of Women

The independence of women seemed rather less unnatural to the Greeks than to other ancients, on account of the fabulous Amazons (whom they believed to be historical), and the partial example afforded by the Spartan women; who, though no less subordinate by law than in other Greek states, were more free in fact, and being trained to bodily exercises in the same manner with men, gave ample proof that they were not naturally disqualified for them.

by *John Stuart Mill*

Isis Unveiled

The dance performed by David round the ark was the "circle-dance" said to have been prescribed by the Amazons for the Mysteries. Such was the dance of the daughters of Shiloh (Judges xxi. 21, 23 et passim), and the leaping of the prophets of Baal (I Kings xviii. 26). It was simply a characteristic of the Sabean worship, for it denoted the motion of the planets round the sun. That the dance was a Bacchic frenzy is apparent. Sistra were used on the occasion, and the taunt of Michael and the king's reply are very expressive. "The king of Israel uncovered himself before his maid-servants as one of the vain (or debauched) fellows shamelessly uncovereth himself." And he retorts: "I will play (act wantonly) before , and I will be yet more vile than this, and I will be base in my own sight." When we remember that David had sojourned among the Tyrians and Philistines, where their rites were common; and that indeed he had conquered that land away from the house of Saul, by the aid of mercenaries from their country, the countenancing and even, perhaps, the introduction of such a Pagan-like worship by the weak "psalmist" seems very natural. David knew nothing of Moses, it seems, and if he introduced the Jehovah-worship it was not in its monotheistic character, but simply as that of one of the many gods of the neighboring nations--a tutelary deity to whom he had given the preference, and chosen among "all other gods."

by *H.P. Blavatsky*

THE KING OF ARGOS

O stranger maids, I may not trust this word,
That ye have share in this our Argive race.
No likeness of our country do ye bear,
But semblance as of Libyan womankind.
Even such a stock by Nilus' banks might grow;
Yea, and the Cyprian stamp, in female forms,
Shows, to the life, what males impressed the same.
And, furthermore, of roving Indian maids
Whose camping-grounds by Aethiopia lie,
And camels burdened even as mules, and bearing
Riders, as horses bear, mine ears have heard;
And tales of flesh-devouring mateless maids
Called Amazons: to these, if bows ye bare,
I most had deemed you like. Speak further yet,
That of your Argive birth the truth I learn.

The Suppliants By *Aeschylus*

Aeschylus lived from about 520 to 456 BC.
He wrote the earliest plays that we have.
Of the 90 plays that he wrote, we have only 7.

Origin of the Amazons

(AN ANCIENT LEGEND OF THE INLAND MOUNTAIN TRIBES.)

1. OF the fierce "Worisiana"
(Such their nation's name)
I can tell the ancient story:
How their warlike strength and glory
First began in shame.
For a chieftain's wife, "To-eyza,"
Faithless dared to be,
Caring nothing for disaster;
Haughty was her lord and master,
Haughtier was she.
At the women's place of bathing,
Thus To-eyza said:
"Some call marriage a protection;
I esteem it base subjection;
Better far be dead!
"Such as we, by parents given,
Nought of love can know;
All our days we spend in sorrow;
'Work to-day,' and 'work to-morrow,'
Ever 'work' — and woe!
"Spurn with me this shameful bondage!
Yon black jaguar see —
See, in that disguise, my lover!
Men like him can soon swim over,
And will set us free!

"Call his name! Let Walyarima
Be our signal cry;
Ye who seek emancipation
From your husbands' domination,
Now behold it nigh!"

II. But three men saw Walyarima
From a neighbouring wood.
Saw and heard, and told the story —
Told their chief, "To-eyborÿri,"
How the matter stood.
To the women, on the morrow,
Calm, the chieftain said,
"Toilsome hunting is before us,
Hunger may be hanging o'er us:
Make cassava bread."
When for roots they all departed,
To the stream he went;
Bade some striplings there "keep moving,"
While, concealed, the rest (approving)
Heard his stern intent.
Those who bathed cried, "Walyarima!"—
Called the hated name,
Spread their long hair on the water;
While each bow lay near for slaughter;

Walyarima came.
As he came, the chief, to meet him,
Dashed into the tide,
Sent his mighty arrow through him;
While the others, swimming to him,
Smote him — as he died.
Grimly, his remains they bore then
To the women's shed—
To the ridge within, suspended,
Left them (for a taunt intended)
Hanging overhead.
Came, in Indian file, the women:
Each her burden bore;
Sternly then their husbands eyed them,
Shrinking from the sights beside them,

On the roof and floor.
Last of all came in To-eyza:
Blood fell on her hand,
Firm she stood, her high head rearing
(E'en the chief admired her bearing)
Beautiful and grand!
Then said he, "We go a-hunting;
Speed, and make the bread —
Bake to-night: we cannot tarry,
Bread for five days we must carry."
"Be it so," she said.
"Bring the meat; and strong paiwári,
More than e'er before;
We your wives will then provide you,
And, that night, will dance beside you,
If we dance no more!"

III.   In the heart of proud To-eyza
Burned a raging flame;
For that drop of blood inspired her,
And the demon power, which fired her.
On the others came.
"For revenge only hearts are burning —
All our hearts," said she.
"Savage insult men provide you!
Ask no questions — I will guide you;
You shall all be free!"

From his hunting came the chieftain;
Laden were his men.
Beasts and birds they brought home twenty,
Smoked or fresh. Then all was plenty —
All was feasting then!
For the women of paiwári
Had abundant store —
All the men had drunk, and rested;
Till the thirsty ones requested
To be served with more.
Then a calabash each woman
Filled up to the brim,
To her husband meekly handed,
(So To-eyza had commanded)
Fatal draught to him!
She had mixed cassava juice there,
Bringing death to all;
Soon, in agony appalling,
Vainly for assistance calling,
Down the warriors fall.
"Now rejoice!" exclaimed To-eyza;
"Women, ye are free!
Nevermore shall husbands rule you,
Beat, oppress, and then befool you,
If you follow me!"
Some, with boys, had fled; the others

Through the midnight hour
Danced, with simulated gladness;
Every bosom filled with madness,
By the demon's power!

IV. Winding through the woods in order,
See a female band,
Hammocks, food, and weapons bearing,
For a weary march preparing,
To some distant land.
To their leader, tall To-eyza,
All obedience pay. —
Sometimes fighting, sometimes flying,
Mainly on their bows relying,
They must win their way.
Many a discontented woman
With them gladly goes.
They proclaim emancipation;
Call themselves the "Woman's nation;"
Husbands treat as foes.
Driving off the men, or slaying,
To their wives they say,
"With your daughters we receive you;
If you keep your sons, we leave you
Here, with them to stay."
On they march, and others follow,
Swelling thus their band;

O'er those females madness creeping;
Like an epidemic, sweeping
Women from the land.
But, meanwhile, the poisoned victims
Kindly friends had found;
Shuddered at the bones before them,
Scared the vultures brooding o'er them;
Placed them in the ground.
Then they followed up those women,
Made the hindmost fly;
Swiftly chased to overtake them,
But their captives none could make them,
They preferred to die.
Soon they came to dark green forests,
Saw their bravest fall;
In their blood the strong men weltered,
Shot by female archers, sheltered
By each leafy wall.
Then they paused; a wise man saying,
"What have we to gain
Of what use to man is woman,
Who regards him as a foeman
Let them march again!"
So those women, still proceeding
Tow'rds the setting sun,
Passing safely through all dangers,

Made a settlement as strangers,
All their journeys done.
There their haughty queen, To-eyza,
Gave them maxims clear:
"We will welcome men as lovers,
If they come as errant rovers;
None must settle here.
"Of their children born amongst us,
Send the boys away;
But whenever girls we bear them,
Joyfully we all must rear them;
Our successors they!"
Ages since have passed; their children
Still observe those laws,
Tell the tale of Walyarima,
'Midst the mountains of Parima:
Still maintain cxtheir cause.

Legends and Myths of the Aboriginal Indians of British Guiana
BY WILLIAM HENRY BRETT

"The Four Princes"

These Princes are Figures seated in Chariots, and thus borne forward. They represent the Vau Forces of the Name in each suit: the Mighty Son of the King and Queen, who realizes the influence of both scales of Force. A Prince, the son of a King and Queen, yet a Prince of Princes, and a King of Kings: an Emperor whose effect is at once rapid (though not so swift as that of the Queen) and enduring. It is, therefore, symbolized by a Figure borne in a Chariot, and clothed in Armour. Yet is his power vain and illusionary, unless set in Motion by his Father and Mother. "The Four Princesses" are the Knaves of the Tarot Pack; The Four Princesses or figures of Amazons, standing firmly of themselves: neither riding upon Horses, nor seated upon Thrones, nor borne in Chariots. They represent the forces of the He final of the Name in each suit, completing the Influences of the other scales: The mighty and potent daughter of a King and Queen: a Princess powerful and terrible: a Queen of Queens --- an Empress --- whose effect combines those of the King, Queen, and Prince, at once violent and permanent; therefore symbolized by a Figure standing firmly by itself, only partially draped, and having but little Armour; yet her power existeth not, save by reason of the others: and then indeed it is mighty and terrible materially, and is the Throne of the Forces of the Spirit. Woe unto whomsoever shall make war upon her, when thus established!

Thelema Texts

(These are texts relating to the philosophy of Thelema, many of them written by the occultist Aleister Crowley.

Such as Diana by the sandie shore
Of swift Eurotas, or on Cynthus greene,
Where all the Nymphes haue her vnwares forlore,
Wandreth alone with bow and arrowes keene,
To seeke her game: Or as that famous Queene
Of Amazons, whom Pyrrhus did destroy,
The day that first of Priame she was seene,
Did shew her selfe in great triumphant ioy,
To succour the weake state of sad afflicted Troy.

The Faerie Queene *by Edmund Spenser*

Stories from the Faerie Queene
by Mary Macleod
(retelling in straightforward modern English Spenser's The Faerie Queene)

RADIGUND, QUEEN OF THE AMAZONS

As Sir Artegall travelled on his way he saw far off a crowd of many people, to whom he hastened, in order to discover the cause of such a large assembly. When he came near he saw a strange sight-a troop of women clad in warlike fashion, with weapons in their hands, as if ready to fight; and in the midst of them he saw a Knight, with both hands pinioned behind him, and round about his neck a halter tight, ready prepared for the gallows. His head was bare and his face covered, so that it was not easy to distinguish him. He went along with a heavy heart, grieved to the soul, and groaning inwardly that he should die so base a death at the hands of women. But they, like merciless tyrants, rejoiced at his misery, and reviled him, and sorely reproached him with bitter taunts and terms of disgrace.

When Artegall, arriving at the place, asked what cause had brought the man to destruction, the women swarmed eagerly around him, meaning to lay their cruel hands on him, and to do him some unexpected mischief. But he was soon aware of their evil mind, and drawing back defeated their intention. He was ashamed to disgrace himself by fighting with women, so he sent Talus to punish them for their rash folly. With a few strokes of his iron flail the latter speedily dispersed their troop, and sent them home to tell a piteous tale of their vain prowess turned to their own injury.

The wretched man doomed to death they left behind them, glad to be quit of them. Talus soon set him at liberty, and released him from his horror at such a shameful death, unfitting a knight, which he dreaded more than loss of life; and uncovering his face, he brought him to his master, who then knew him at once.

"Sir Terpin!" cried Artegall. "Hapless man, what are you doing here? Have you lost yourself and your senses? Or have you, who can boast of subduing men, yielded to the oppression of women? Or what other deadly misfortune has fallen on you, that you have run so foolishly far astray as to lead yourself to your own destruction?"

The man was so confused, partly with shame, partly with dismay, that he stood lost in astonishment, and could find little to say in excuse.

"You may justly term me hapless, who am brought to this shame, and am to-day made the scorn of knighthood," was his only answer. "But who can escape Fate? The work of Heaven's will surpasses human thought."

"True," said Sir Artegall, "but faulty men often attribute their own folly to Fate, and lay on Heaven the guilt of their own crimes. But tell me, Sir Terpin--and do not let your misery daunt you--how you fell into this state."

"Since you needs will know my shame," said the Knight, "and all the ill which has lately chanced to me, I will briefly relate it, and do not turn my misfortune to my blame.

"Being desirous, as all knights are, to try deeds of arms through hard adventures, and to hunt after fame and honour, I heard a report which flew far abroad that a proud Amazon lately bade defiance to all brave knights, and wrought them all the villainy her malice could devise, putting some to shame, and doing many of them to death.

"The cause of her hate is for the sake of a Knight called Bellodant the Bold, whom a short time ago she liked greatly, and tried in every way to attract; but finding nothing of any avail, her love turned to hatred, and for his sake she vowed to do all the ill she could to other knights,--which vow she now fulfils.

"For all those knights whom by force or guile she subdues she treats shamefully. First she despoils them of their armour, and clothes them in women's garments; then with threats she compels them to work to earn their food--to spin, to card, to sew, to wash, to wring. She gives them nothing to eat but bread and water, or some such feeble food, to disable them from attempting revenge.

"But if with manly disdain any of them withstand her insolent commands, she causes them to be immediately hanged on that gibbet over there, in which condition I stood just now; for being conquered by her in fight, and put to the base service of her band, I chose rather to die than to live that shameful life, unworthy of a knight."

"What is the name of that Amazon?" asked Artegall. "And where, and how far hence does she live?"

"Her name is called Radigund," replied Sir Terpin, "a princess of great power, and greater pride, Queen of the Amazons, well tried in arms and sundry battles, which she has achieved with great success, and which have won her much glory and fame."

"Now, by my faith," said Sir Artegall, "I will not rest till I have tested her power, and avenged the shame that she shows to knights. Therefore, Sir Terpin, throw from you those squalid clothes, the pattern of despair, and go with me, that you may see and know how Fortune will repair your ruined name and knighthood, whose praise she would tarnish."

Sir Terpin joyfully threw off his iron fetters, and eagerly prepared to guide the way to the dwelling of the Amazon, which was not more than a mile or two distant--a goodly and a mighty city, called after her own name Radigone.

On their arrival they were immediately espied by the watchman, who warned all the city of the appearance of three warlike persons, of whom one seemed like a Knight fully armed, and the other two likely to prove dangerous. The people ran at once to put on their armour, swarming in a cluster like bees, and before long their Queen herself, looking half like a man, came forth into the crowd, and began to set them in array.

And now the Knights, being arrived near, beat upon the gates to enter in; threatening the porter, who scorned them for being so few, to tear him to pieces if they won the city. When Radigund beard them her heart was torn with rage. She bade her people to unbar the gates at once, and to make way for the knights with well-prepared weapons.

As soon as the gates were set open the Knights pressed forward to make an entrance, but midway they were met by a sharp shower of arrows, which stopped them. Then all the mob attacked them savagely, heaping strokes so fast on every side, and with such a hail of arrows, that the Knights could not withstand them. But Radigund herself, when she espied Sir Terpin freed from her cruel doom, was suddenly seized with a fit of fury, and flying at him like a lioness, smote him so fiercely that he fell to the ground. Then she leaped to him, and placed her foot on his neck.

When Sir Artegall saw the Knight's peril, he sprang at once to his rescue, and assailed Radigund with such vigour that he drove her back. For a moment she was stunned, but as soon as she collected her senses she turned on Sir Artegall, half-mad with revengeful anger and pride, for she had never suffered such a rebuff. But before they could meet in fight her maidens flocked round her so fast that they parted them, in spite of their valour, and kept them far asunder. But amongst the others the fight lasted till the evening.

And all the while the great Iron Man sorely vexed the Amazons with his strange weapon, to

which they had never been accustomed in war. He chased and outran them, and broke their bows, and spoilt their shooting, so that not one of them all dared to go near him. They scattered like sheep before a wolf, and fled before him through all the fields and valleys.

But when the daylight grew dim with the shadows of night, Radigund, with the sound of a trumpet, caused her people to cease fighting, and gathering them to the gate of the city, made them all enter, and had the weak and wounded conveyed in, before she would retreat herself.

When the field was thus empty and all things quiet, Sir Artegall, weary with toil and travel, caused his pavilion to be richly prepared in full view of the city gate. He himself, together with Sir Terpin, rested here in safety all that night; but Talus was accustomed, in times of jeopardy, to keep a nightly watch for fear of treachery.

Radigund, full of heart-gnawing grief for the rebuke she had met that day, could take no rest nor relief, but tossed about in her mind in what way she could revenge her disgrace. Then she resolved to try her fortune in single fight herself, rather than see her people destroyed, as she had seen that day.

She called to her a trusty maid, named Clarinda, whom she thought fittest for the business, and said to her--

"Go, damsel, quickly; get ready to do the message which I shall tell you, Go you to the stranger Knight who yesterday drove us to such distress; tell him that to-morrow I will fight with him, and try in a fair field which is the mightier.

"But these conditions you must propound to him--that if I vanquish him he shall obey my law, and ever be bound to do my bidding And so will I, if he vanquish me, whatever he shall like to do or say. Go straight, and take with you as witness six of your companions of the highest rank; and carry with you wine and rich delicacies, and bid him eat: henceforth he shall often sit hungry."

The damsel instantly obeyed, and putting all in readiness went forth to the town gate, where, sounding a trumpet loudly from the wall, she sent warning to the warrior Knights. Then Talus, issuing from the tent, took his way fearlessly to the wall, to know what that sounding of the trumpet meant, whereupon the damsel called to him, and explained that she wished to parley with his lord.

Then he conducted them at once to his master, who gave them a cordial greeting, and to whom they told their message, word for word. Sir Artegall, gladly accepting it, entertained them with fitting courtesy, and gave them rich and handsome gifts. So they turned their steps homeward again, but Artegall went back to rest, that he might be fresher against the next day's fight.

THE BATTLE OF QUEEN RADIGUND AND BRITOMART

That night Britomart spent in the great Temple of Isis, which was dedicated in days of old to the worship of justice. Here in her sleep she had a wondrous vision, which at first filled her with dread. But when she described it next morning to the priests in the Temple, they told her that her dream had a good meaning, and that everything would end well. Greatly relieved to hear this, she bestowed rich rewards on the priests, and made royal gifts of gold and silver to the Temple. Then taking leave of them, she went forward to seek her love, never resting and never relenting till she came to the land of the Amazons.

When news of her approach was brought to Radigund she was filled with courage and glee instead of being dismayed. Glad to hear of fighting, of which she had now had none for a long time, she bade them open the gates boldly, so that she might see the face of her new foe; but when they told her of the Iron Man who had lately slain her people, she bade them hold them shut.

So there outside the gate, as seemed best, her pavilion was pitched, in which brave Britomart rested herself, while Talus watched at her door all night. All night, likewise, those of the town, in terror, kept good watch and ward upon their wall.

The next morning, as soon as it was dawn, the warlike Amazon peeped out of her bower, and caused a shrill trumpet to sound to warn her foe to hasten to the battle. Britomart, who had long been awake and arrayed for contest, immediately stepped haughtily from the pavilion, ready for the fight, and on the other side her foe soon appeared.

But before they lifted hand, Radigund began to propound the strict conditions with which she always fettered her foes--that Britomart should serve her as she had bound the rest to do. At this, Britomart frowned sternly, in disdain of such indignity, and would no longer parley, but bade them sound the advance, for she would be tied by no other terms than those prescribed by the laws of chivalry.

The trumpets sounded, and they rushed together with greedy rage, smiting with their falchions; neither sought to shun the other's stroke, but both savagely hacked and hewed, furious as a tiger - and a lioness fighting over the same prey. So long they fought that all the grassy floor was trampled with blood. At last Radigund, having espied some near advantage, let drive at Britomart with all her might, thus taunting her with savage scorn--

"Bear this token to the man whom you love so dearly, and tell him you gave your life for his sake!"

The cruel stroke glanced on Britomart's shoulder plate, and bit to the bone, so that she could hardly hold up her shield for the smart of it. Yet she soon avenged it, for the furious pain gave her fresh force, and she smote Radigund so rudely on the helmet that it pierced to the very brain, and felled her to the ground, where with one stroke Britomart killed her.

When Radigund's warrior band saw this dreadful sight they all fled into the town, and left Britomart sole victor. But they could not retreat so fast but that Talus could overtake the foremost. Pressing through the mob to the gate, he entered in with them, and then began a piteous slaughter; for all who came within reach of his iron flail were soon beyond the skill of any doctor.

Then the noble Conqueror herself came in, and though she had sworn a vow of revenge, yet when she saw the heaps of dead bodies slain by Talus, her heart was torn with pity, and she bade him slack his fury. Having thus stayed the massacre, she inquired for the iron prison where her love lay captive. Breaking it open with indignant rage, she entered, and went all over it; when she saw the strange and horrible sight of the men dressed up in womanish garb, her heart groaned with compassion for such unmanly and disgraceful misery.

When at last she came to her own Knight, whom the like disguise had no less disfigured, abashed with shame she turned aside her head, and then with pity and tender words she tried to comfort him. She caused the unsightly garments to be immediately taken off, and in their stead sought for other raiment, of which there was great store, as well as bright armour reft from many a noble knight whom the proud Amazon had subdued. When Sir Artegall was clad anew in this apparel Britomart's spirits revived, and she rejoiced in his gallant appearance.

They remained for awhile in the city of Queen Radigund, so that Sir Artegall might recover his strength, and Britomart be healed of her wounds. During this time Britomart reigned as a Princess, and changed all the order of government. The women were deposed from the rule which they had usurped, and true justice was dealt them, so that, worshipping Britomart as a goddess, they all admired her wisdom and listened to her teaching. All those knights who had long been hidden in captivity, she freed from their thraldom, and made magistrates of the city, giving them great wealth and authority. And in order that they should always remain faithful, she made them swear fealty to Artegall.

As the latter Knight was now fully recovered, he proposed to proceed upon the first adventure which had called him forth, the release of the: Lady Irene from the villain Grantorto. Very sad and sorrowful was Britomart at his departure, yet wisely moderated her own grief, seeing that his honour, which she put above all things, was much concerned in carrying out that adventure. For a little while after lie had gone she remained there in the city, but finding her misery increase with his absence, and hoping that change of air and place would somewhat ease her sorrow, she too departed, to appease her anguish in travel.

According to assorted Greek histories and myths, the Amazons of the Thermodon valley made war against the peoples of Asia Minor for many decades and perhaps even centuries until finally a man was able to pull out a victory against them. The Greek hero (or in this case anti-hero) who took this distinction was Bellerophon, who arrived at the land of the Amazons following a circuitous series of adventures.

Bellerophon was born to Glaucus, the King of Corinth, and his wife Eurynome. However, the story goes that Glaucus was actually unable to conceive a child, and Eurynome mated with the god

of the sea, Poseidon, in order to bare her son. Bellerophon considered himself the son of a god, as did many others, and his unusually handsome good looks as well as his strength and intelligence seemed to bear out this belief.

The charmed young demigod's life began to go sour however, when he accidentally caused the death of his brother, Deliades. In humiliation, Bellerophon fled to Argos, where he threw himself at the mercy of King Proteus, asking him to allow him to remain with him and atone for his sin. Proteus could not refuse this request, as to do so would be against the code of Greek behavior which put hospitality close to godliness, and Bellerophon was welcomed into the king's household.

Proteus' wife, Queen Antea, became infatuated with the handsome Bellerophon and let it be known to him. When Bellerophon refused her attentions and rejected her advances, Antea was incensed and turned against him. She falsely reported to her husband that Bellerophon had tried to rape her, knowing that this accusation would foil the young man's efforts to purify himself of his sins and that the king would surely put him to death.

Proteus was indeed furious at Bellerophon, but those same laws of hospitality forbade him to kill a guest. Instead, the king forged a plan to have Bellerophon murdered by someone other than himself. Antea was a princess of Lycia, and her father Iobates was still on the throne there. Proteus sent Bellerophon to his father-in-law telling him he was to go as a messenger and deliver a letter to Iobates. When Bellerophon arrived in Lycia he was again greeted with warm Greek hospitality, and nine days of wining and dining were afforded him before Iobates asked to see what letter had been sent from his son-in-law. When he finally read the message he was shocked to see that it bate him kill the messenger! Iobates, too, however, was bound by the rules of hospitality and since Bellerophon was now his guest, he would not risk the wrath of the gods by killing him. Iobates instead schemed to punish Bellerophon by setting before him three frightening and difficult tasks. The first was to kill a terrifying fire-breathing monster, the Chimera, which terrorized the people and killed every living creature in its path. It had the head of a lion on the body of a goat, and the tail of a snake. Bellerophon succeeded in killing the Chimera and went on to the second task which was to defeat the fierce army of the Solymi. This too, Bellerophon accomplished.

While fasting and praying for help in defeating the monster, Bellerophon had a vision – a golden horse's bridle. When he woke the next morning, the bridle was actually on the ground next to him, which he took as a sign that the goddess Athena had answered his prayers for guidance. When Bellerophon later saw Pegasus, a winged horse, he knew the bridle was meant for him, and he gently tamed the marvelous creature, slipping the bridle over Pegasus' neck easily. After this Bellerophon and Pegasus were inseparable, and the horse was with him when he faced the third task put to Bellerophon by Iobates - to conquer the Amazons.

We don't know many details about the clash between Bellerophon and the Amazon warriors, but in the end the women were no match for the Greek and his flying horse.

When Bellerophon returned to Iobates after his rousing victory over the Amazons he expected a hero's welcome. When it became apparent that Iobates was sending him to more and more dangerous situations in hopes that he might carry out his son in law's wish to kill him, Bellerophon confided to Iobates what had actually occurred with his daughter. The king believed the young man, and even rewarded him with his other daughter in marriage.

Several ancient authors have provided us with the gripping tale of a second Greek hero, Heracles, and his adventures with the Amazons. Heracles was a prominent Greek god who began his life as a mortal man whose father was none other than the Father of the Olympian Gods himself – the great Zeus. Even the most powerful of gods were known to be attracted at times to mortal women, and Zeus was no exception. He lusted after Alcmene, the wife of Amphitryon, King of Thebes. Alcmene was not inclined to return Zeus's affections however, so the great god had to resort to trickery to win a night of love with her. He disguised himself as her husband, and came to her under the cover of darkness, which worked like a charm, and Alcmene willingly mated with him. Magically, the sky remained dark three times longer than on an ordinary night, and when dawn

finally broke, Alcmene had been impregnated by Zeus. By the time she discerned what had taken place it was too late – the child Heracles had been conceived.

The goddess Hera was Zeus's rightful wife, and she was incensed with anger upon hearing of her husband's latest extra-marital escapade. Hera was already known for intense jealousy toward her husband's cohorts and this time she vowed to make sure that Alcmene would not be able to carry the pregnancy to term. Hera dispatched witches to place spells on the woman that would cause her to miscarry the child. The witches' efforts were for naught however, and in due time Alcmene gave birth to twins – Heracles, the son of Zeus, and Iphicles, the son of her husband, King Amphitryon.

When Heracles emerged from the womb a strapping flesh and blood child, albeit a mortal child, Hera's anger knew no bounds. The infant's robust size and red hair could point only to his being the offspring of her husband, Zeus. Hera was determined that the child not survive to his first birthday. She sent two serpents to the twins' nursery with orders to kill both the infants, and the serpents tried mightily to crush Heracles, only to be met with their own death at the hands of the powerful baby. He saved his twin brother as well, who escaped with only some injuries.

Hera did not give up, but she bided her time as meanwhile Heracles grew into a man. His strength and bravery were almost inhuman in proportion, and he moved away from Thebes at the request of Amphitryon. This was perhaps in order to distance himself from normal society and at the same time make sure that the surrounding countryside was rendered void of dangerous beasts, which he killed with his bare hands to keep Thebes safe. When Megrea, a princess of Thebes, agreed to become Heracles wife, Heracles was a happy man, and his joy increased with the birth of each of his own two sons soon after. Hera had remained in the background for a while, but her jealousy had not been assuaged, and the worst was yet to come. Once he was ensconced in his serene and happy life, Hera caused Heracles to become mentally deranged. In a fit of madness he killed his children. When he returned to sanity and realized what he had done Heracles was deeply grieved and remorseful. He left Megrea, fearing he might harm her as well, and his friend Theseus begged him to go to the Delphi oracle and ask what to do next. The priestess at Delphi told Heracles to throw himself at the mercy of Eurystheus, who was at that time King of Thebes, and beg him to set before him tasks with which he could perform in order to redeem himself from his horrible crime.

Hera urged Eurystheus to punish Heracles harshly, and Eurystheus obliged, though he stopped short at having Heracles killed. Instead, he assigned him twelve "labors", one more terrible and terrifying than the next, involving the capture and killing of terrible beasts and monsters and other "impossible" missions which only a man of unsurpassed strength and cunning could accomplish. The ninth of these labors was to bring back the Girdle of the Amazon Queen. And here Heracles' Amazon adventure begins.

The Amazons of the River Thermodon area were ruled by Queen Hippolyte who was said to be the daughter of the war-god Ares. Ares had gifted Hippolyte with a special armored belt to signify her unmatched prowess in battle. The belt was used as a sheath for Hippolyte's sword and a place to hang her shield. Some authors call the belt a "girdle" and point out its significance to the Amazons for symbolic reasons other than those related to Hippolyte's warrior status. The girdle was a sacred symbol of the Amazons' virginity, and this particular girdle of Hippolyte was also supposed to have had magical powers.

Heracles set out with an army of supporters, including his loyal friend Theseus, who had by then become the

Athenian king. He knew that to come face to face with the Amazonian army was to be a dangerous mission indeed. Heracles' party sailed party set sail in a fleet of strong ships, and crossed the Aegean, on through the Black Sea, until they reached the mouth of the River Thermodon. The Greek force remained intact and unmolested for the duration of the journey and when they reached the river they sailed upstream toward the Amazon city of Themyscira.

The ancient authors supply us with several versions as to what took place. According to Appolodorus, Heracles docked at Themyscira and was met at his boat by Hippolyte who greeted him in a friendly manner and inquired as to why he had come. When he answered that he'd been dispatched by King Eurystheus who desired the girdle of an Amazon queen for his daughter, Hippolyte, who was taken by Heracles' charms, agreed to gift him with her girdle.

All might have ended peacefully were it not for the vengeful Hera who still harbored hatred toward Heracles. Seeing a chance for Heracles to finally meet his end at the hands of the mighty Amazons, Hera decided to stir up trouble. She disguised herself as an Amazon, and ran among the women shouting that the Greeks were there to carry off their queen. The Amazon warriors responded to Hera's warnings and made ready for battle by arming themselves and mounting their steeds. When Heracles saw the approaching horses bearing women in full armor he jumped to the conclusion that Hippolyte had deceived him, letting him believe that she would willingly give up the girdle while all the while the Amazons made ready to attack him. He immediately put the hapless Hippolyte to death, and went out with his men to fight the warriors Hera had set against him.

Diodorus and others tell a slightly different tale whereby the Amazons at this time were ruled by two sister queens. Antiope was the "home queen" and Orithya was the "war queen". At the time of Heracles arrival Orithya was away with her armies engaged in some distant battle, and it was Antiope who greeted the Greek intruders. Antiope was informed of Heracles impending arrival with very little notice and did not have time to dispatch messengers to Orithya and call her home. Heracles demanded the girdle (which in this version belongs to Antiope) and had she agreed to give it up this would have symbolized total capitulation of the Amazons to the

Greeks. Antiope stiffly refused, and battle ensued.

In both versions at this point the Amazons fought valiantly against the Greeks, but without benefit of their warrior queen's leadership and with their best fighters being abroad, they were at a terrible disadvantage. Heracles wore his lion skin, which rendered him almost impenetrable, and one by one he slayed the Amazons who bravely engaged him in hand to hand combat. He killed eleven Amazon officers single-handedly. Aella, Philippis, Ainippe, Prothoe, and Asteria, Melanippe, Hipsipile, Deianeira, Tecmessa, Alcippe, and Eriobea were among the dead.

Other authors make no mention of a battle at this juncture, saying that when Heracles thought Hippolyte had betrayed him he simply killed her, took the girdle from her person, and sailed for home. Apollonius offered another story by which Heracles did not kill Hippolyte, but captured her sister Melanippe (also called Antiope) and demanded Hippolyte's girdle in return for Melanippe's freedom.

According to Diodorus, Heracles captured Antiope alive, and forced her to give up her girdle. He then turned her over to his friend Theseus who carried her off to Athens.

It is unclear whether Antiope and Hippolyte refer to two separate persons or whether they are perhaps two renderings of the same queen.

While most authors place Theseus together with Heracles when the pair landed in Themyscira, there are also versions, Plutarch's included, that claim Theseus acted independently of Heracles, having met Hippolyte(or Antiope) on an excursion of his own. The queen came willingly to his ship bearing friendly gifts and Theseus fell for her charms, setting sail for Greece with Hippolyte (Antiope) aboard as his future bride.

"Dahomey, a small kingdom on the Slave Coast, has sufficient open country, to allow of cooperation and aggressive military operations. It is said that this state at one time had an army of 50,000 mien and its terrible fighting Amazons of 3,000 women were no inconsiderable military force... This Dahomey kingdom flourished for centuries and was one of the most powerful allies of the slave traders during the seventeenth and eighteenth centuries. It is supposed that this country alone, at the height of the slave trade, delivered an annual quota of fifteen thousand slaves, most of which were captured from neighbouring tribes."

W. D. Weatherford, The Negro from Africa to America

Amazons in Africa

In war time, even now, strong women on both sides act as scouts. They know that they will not be killed, so go before the main body fearlessly spying upon the enemy. As soon as the first sign of the latter is seen they cry out to warn their own men, and then run aside so as not to be in the way.

At times a band of Amazons comes across and captures a single foeman. Then these women, usually so gentle and kindly, seem to change their whole nature. They fall upon the luckless man, bind, and often cruelly wound him; then hand him over in triumph to be slain by the men of their own party.

Perhaps the most important service rendered by the women of the tribe in time of war is the carrying out of the secret rites decreed by ancient law for the burial of a warrior... "When a man in the prime of life is cut off in battle, the body is carried home to the dead man's town by wedded women who are his next of kin. No man may touch the corpse. Weeping and singing sad songs, it is borne by their gentle hands to a place of thick bush called owok afai--the forest of those slain by sudden death... No maiden may be present at these rites; only to wives may such sad mysteries be revealed."

D. AMAURY TALBOT. WOMAN'S MYSTERIES OF A PRIMITIVE PEOPLE

The myths about the Amazons not just became a part of epic poetry but also were a source for creative activity in arts. Battling women is so unusual and exciting imaginary show that it attracted artists of all the times and Amazons and other ancient female warriors have been portrayed by famous artists.

Quintus Smyrnus probably gives the best rendering of this last legend, though he adds certain marvels. According to him, Penthesilea is moved not so much by hatred against the Greeks as from a personal grief, she having accidentally killed her sister while out hunting. So

> "Her crime to expiate, with her sword
> To offer victims to the Furies dire,
> Who, tho' unseen, pursu'd her to avenge
> Her sister's blood; for with unwearied speed
> They chase the guilty, tracking all their steps."

Spurred on by this terrible need for atoning by offering human victims to the ghost of the dead and to the outraged deities, Penthesilea goes forth with her twelve companions, and is welcomed by Priam. On the fatal morn,

> *"when Aurora, rosy-ankled, smil'd,*
> *Penthesilea left her couch, and cloth'd*
> *Her limbs in armour sheen, the gift of Mars;*
> *First to her snowy legs she fitted close*
> *The golden greaves, and on her tender breast*
> *Bound the strong plate of variegated mail.*
> *Then from her shoulder the huge sword she slung*
> *Proudly, its sheath all exquisitely wrought*
> *With ivory and silver. Next she took*
> *Her crescent buckler, like the horned moon,*
> *When, gleaming o'er the waves, she climbs the sky*

With half-replenished lamp. Her helmet last,
Its nodding crest beropt with gold, she plac'd
Upon her head. In this array she shone
Refulgent, as the forky fires that Jove
Hurls to earth, the red vaunt-couriers
Of the big rain-drops, and the roaring winds.
In her left band, behind the shield, she bore
Two jav'lins snatched in haste, and in her right
An axe with double edge, which Discord gave
To the maiden's great defence in war."

Then she hurries to the fray, carrying slaughter among the Greeks, and at last espying Achilles and Ajax, she flies to meet them, and after the inevitable war of words, she is slain by Achilles, who, stooping to remove her armour,

"felt exceeding grief
As on the body of the maid he gaz'd,
Mourning her not less than for the death
Of his belov'd Patroclus."

Quintus adds that Mars rushed down from Olympus, alighting on Mount Ida, which rocked and streamed with fire, and the war god would have attacked the Greeks had he not been restrained by the thunder and lightning of angered Jove.

PLUTARCH MENTIONS:

...in the relief of the battle of the Amazons, which is represented on the shield of the goddess, he carved a figure representing himself as a bald old man, lifting up a stone with both hands... he introduced a particularly fine likeness of Pericles fighting an Amazon. The position of the hand, which holds a spear in front of Pericle's face, seems to have been ingeniously contrived to conceal the resemblance, but it can still be seen quite plainly from either side.

" ... As regards the Amazons, the same stories are told now as in early times, though they are marvelous and beyond belief. For instance, who could believe that a an army of women, or a city, or a tribe, could ever be organized without men, and not only be organized, but make inroads upon the territory of other people, and not only overpower the peoples near them to the extent of advancing as far as what is now Ionia, but even send an expedition acrossthe sea as far as Attica? For this is to say that the men of those times were women and that the women were men."

Strabo, Geography (11.5.3)

For the real Amazons of Greek mythology are not of dust or decay, but of marble friezes and graceful amphoras and poets nodding upon grassy hillocks in Ionia. They are shining young women in shining armor, living with a horse between their legs and arrogantly scrawling the supremacy of their sex on the unending scroll of the wind.

D. Sobol

The Amazons existed; their tribes were a basic primitive form of female social pattern; and if there are so many legends of felmale-only islands, it is because Amazon tribes often lived on islands. When these Amazon societies were destroyed by male supremacist societies, lesbians became the heiresses of an ever-menaced culture that had to move from islands of stone and sand to psycho-spiritual shelters, to "mind-drifting islands."

B. Weinbaum

Quintus Smyrnus in his account of the struggle between the Greeks and Amazons before Troy. The warrior feeling is expressed by Hippodamia, who, excited by the brave deeds of Penthesilea and her companions, calls upon the Trojan maids and matrons--

"Come, friends, let us too in our hearts conceive
A martial spirit such as now inflames
Our warriors fighting for their native walls;
For not in strength are we inferior much
To men; the same our eyes, our limbs the same;
One common light we see, one air we breathe;
Nor different is the food we eat. What then
Denied to us hath Heaven on man bestowed?
O let us hasten to the glorious war!"

But Theano, "for her prudence famed," deprecates such a move--

"Till the foe hath closely girt our towers
We shall not need the aid of female hands."

The Amazons in Athens

When Orithya returned from her distant campaign she was met with the news of Heracles' mission. According to the most frequently told version, Hippolyte had had been carried off to Athens by Theseus who wanted to marry her. When their third sister Menaloppe explained to Orithya what had happened Orithya turned to Sagillus, the Scythian king, for assistance against the Greek threat, convincing them that he shared a common enemy with the Amazons. Sagillus responded by sending his son, Penasagoras to their aid.

Orithya vowed to set the considerable Amazon might against the even mightier Greeks and to bring back their captured queen. She raised a solid army, and marched them down the coast of the Black Sea and crossed over at a narrow strait which was frozen over in winter. On their way the Amazons erected a temple to Ares on an island. They marched by way of Thessaly, and on their arrival in Minerva they set up camp. From this base Orithya sent word to Theseus of her demands. She asked for the swift return of Hippolyte and the sacred girdle of Ares. The Amazon messengers left their audience with Theseus empty-handed, however, and Theseus began preparations for a showdown. His first act was to make a sacrifice to the Goddess of Fear, whose temple was never used except in times of dire emergency. Theseus beseeched the god to protect the Greeks against the frightful female invaders and to punish those who would march against Athens. He then led the first attack against the Amazons.

An extended battle took place in which each side fought with all its might and wits. Attack after attack ended in stand-off between the sides. Then, the Athenians made a decisive stand, coming from the Palladium and the Lyceum. It has been noted by numerous writers that this turning point in favor of the Athenians was not easy to accomplish. The Greeks had to fight hard and long to turn the tide of the battle against the Amazons. There were numerous casualties on both sides, as each side refused to let up and fought desperately with all of its skill. The Greeks, led by Theseus, engaged the Amazons in fierce hand to hand combat, which finally proved too much for the women, and they retreated to their camp in Minerva.

While the Amazons resting in their camp – tired but not entirely defeated – Hippolyte tried to mediate between her husband and his enemies, her own people. A truce was hammered out, and an oath of peace between the two nations was sworn. After the dead from both sides had been put to honorable rest, a structure was erected to commemorate the treaty, called Oath House. The Amazons marched safely back through Greece toward home. It had been four months since they set out from the Thermodon.

One story claims that Hippolyte joined her comrades for the march back to Thermodon, but perished and was buried in Megara and a great tomb erected to her memory. Plutarch tells a bit of a different story, stating that Antiope (Hippolyte) was killed during a battle when she tried to shield Theseus from an oncoming arrow. Another myth asserts that after the Amazons departed, Theseus took another wife, Phaedra. Hippolyte's jealousy was ignited and she was killed when she led a band of Amazon warriors back to Athens to the wedding feast and disrupted the festivities.

Theseus had a son, Hipploytus, who was born at around this time. It is unclear whether the mother of Hippolytus was Antiope, Hippolyte, or Phaedra, and whether the Amazon wife was even alive at the time of the birth.

As the Amazons marched toward home, they erected statues and temples along with way in thanksgiving. They looked up on their retreat as having left under truce, and did not consider themselves a vanquished army. They marched by way of Thessaly again, and in Thrace they dedicated a new Amazon settlement.

Apparently they were too ashamed to return to Themyscira without being able to report decisive victory over the Athenians.

Penthesilea and Achilles

In the Iliad, Homer briefly mentions that the Amazons took part in the Trojan War, siding with King Priam against the Greeks and being defeated roundly by their hero Achilles. This would have taken place approximately five hundred years before the Labor of Heracles and the marriage of Theseus to an Amazon queen. A more extensive tale is woven by Arktinos in his Aithiopis, a sequel to Homer's work. This story has been passed down in truncated form however, since a good portion of Aithiopis has been lost over the years. Quintus of Smyrna later wrote an involved account of these events in his Greek epic narrative describing the Trojan War, giving us most of what we now know of a most unusual romantic and tragic affair.

The story begins with the birth of the extraordinarily beautiful Helena. Zeus, the greatest of the Gods, fathered Helena when in the form of a swan he seduced the beautiful mortal woman Leda. Leda's husband believed himself to be the father of Helen, and was extremely protective of his daughter in every way. Before he would allow her to marry he extracted an agreement, signed by all of the Greek generals which stated that the entire Greek army vowed to uphold Helena's honor if it should ever prove necessary. This vow thus sealed, Helena was given in marriage to Menaleus, King of Sparta.

Meanwhile, Priam, King of Troy, had a son, Paris. To Paris fell the difficult job of choosing the "fairest of them all" at a gathering of lovely and competitive goddesses including Aphrodite, Athena, and Hera. Paris came bearing a golden apple engraved with the title "the fairest", and each woman tried as she might to get him to bestow it upon her. In the end, Aphrodite, goddess of love attained the prize when she bribed Paris with the promise of none other than the notoriously lovely Helena.

Paris eagerly traveled to Sparta to claim his reward, and when he met Helena their love turned out to be mutual. While Menaleus was away, Paris spirited Helena out of Sparta and returned with her to Troy. Soon the Spartans were in hot pursuit, but the lovers sped away from them, attaining the walls of Troy safely. When Menaleus returned from his travels to find his wife had been abducted, he, might be expected, did not take this turn of events lightly. He traveled forthwith to Troy, accompanied by his friend Odysseus, King of Ithaca, to demand the return of his queen.

When the Prince of Troy flatly refused to give Helen up, the Spartans recalled the earlier agreement and demanded that it be upheld, calling forth the Greek forces which aligned against Troy making ready to invade in order to "liberate" Helena. Thus began a long and bloody war.

The mighty Greek warrior Achilles was the hero of Homer's tale of the war against the Trojans. Achilles was the son of a mortal man and the Nereid Thetis. In an effort to make her son immune to mortal dangers, Thetis held the infant Achilles by the heel and dipped him into the waters of the River Styx, waters said to have the ability to confer indestructibility to anything anointed by them. The waters did not make Achilles immortal, but they seemed to have gifted him with an extraordinary strength and courage, which he exhibited later as a warrior for Greece at Troy.

The war raged on for almost ten years before the events concerning the Amazons took place. Both sides were exhausted yet still fighting insistently and brutally. Achilles had distinguished himself as an indispensable hero to the Greeks. The undefeatable Achilles always fought with his intimate friend and confidant Petroklas at his side, and the two were as close as brothers. With Achilles in the lead the Greeks captured city after Trojan city, always taking the spoils of war as they went. In one place Achilles chose for himself a war prize in the form of a woman, Briseis. Soon after however, the Achaean King Agamemnon who headed the campaign against the Trojans, took a fancy to Briseis himself and ordered Achilles to give her up to him. Having no choice, Achilles relinquished his mistress, but he was deeply insulted and humiliated by having had such a request put upon him. He demonstrated his fury by ceasing to participate in any further military activities.

With Achilles on strike from the Greek forces the war took a turn in favor of the Trojans. Hector, the militarily talented son of Priam, led his forces brilliantly and was hailed as a magnificent hero. The Greeks were desperate to get Achilles back into the fray, knowing that only he could stand up to the great Trojan prince and his troops. Achilles was offered many a bribe and incentive, and Agamemnon even offered the return of Briseis, but the hero stood firm in his refusal to step back into battle.

Under pressure from the Greeks and in a show of fatally poor judgment, Achilles decided to give his own armor to Petroklas and have him ride into war in his friend's place. At first this seemed a good plan. Petroklas was a good soldier, and wearing Achilles' armor he proved himself quite valuable to the Greeks, emerging victorious time and again. It looked as if the tides of the war had turned, until that inevitable fateful day when Petroklas met his match in Hector. As Petroklas rode toward Hector, the Trojan prince recognized the armor, and believed he was finally coming fact to fact with the great hero, Achilles. In a fierce hand to hand battle, Hector gained the upper hand, and killed Petroklas, only realizing when he removed Achilles' armor from corpse that he had felled a different Greek warrior.

Odysseus

When the body of his friend was born back to the Greek camp by his comrades in arms, Achilles was overcome with deep grief and guilt over the death of his loyal and brave friend. The demise of Petroklas was perhaps the only event which could have lured Achilles back into the war, but now his hatred of Hector overshadowed his resentment of Agamemnon and he was ready to face the Trojans once more. This time Achilles would be fighting to avenge the death of the faithful companion who had marched into danger at his behest. Spiritually broken but mentally and physically prepared, Achilles donned a new set of armor ordered by his mother Thetis, and prepared for him by the Greek artisan Hephaestus.

Achilles' new armor was colorful and spectacular. Hector recognized the hero immediately, and approached him with a request before the two came out fighting. The Trojan asked that whoever should be victorious might return the body of his felled enemy to his people. Achilles scoffed at this, and refused to make any such oath. Blinded by his grief over Petroklas, Achilles had no inclination whatever to be gentlemanly toward his mortal foe. Indeed, Achilles fought Hector viciously until the latter lay vanquished at his feet, and even then his anger was not assuaged. Achilles removed Hector's armor, and amid protests had Hector's body tied to the chariot which carried him charging back to the Greek camp.

King Priam would not abide knowing that his son's body lay vilified in the enemy compound. He risked his life by going secretly to the Greeks to beg for the release of Hector's corpse. Priam found the Greek hero in a different frame of mind altogether, since Achilles had finally spent his pent up rage and hatred. He was actually quite respectful as he handed Hector back to the King. Not only did he return the younger man's body, but Achilles treated Priam with the honor due any king and the consideration due any father mourning a son.

All of this took place during the time when the Amazons were ruled by Queen Penthesilea, a daughter of Ares who possessed a rare and special beauty. Penthesilea had already proven herself a fierce and brave warrior, and had killed quite a number of Greeks. When the final year of the Trojan War began the queen was presently in her own tragic drama. Penthesilea went out hunting with her sister Hippolyte, as was their usual routine, and seeing a hart in the distance, the queen took aim with her javelin, expecting to fell the animal. This time, however, it was Hippolyte who called out in pain, and died from wounds accidentally inflicted by her sister's weapon.

Penthesilea was inconsolable in her grief and guilt over her sister's death, and she desperately prayed for a way to purify herself after such a horrible, even if unintentional act. It was in this state that the messengers dispatched by Priam found her. They had come to beg the Amazon queen for assistance in the continuing war against the Greeks and the great Achilles. Priam greatly feared that the Trojans would not be able to mount an adequate defense now that the great warrior Hector was gone and saw an alliance with the Amazons as his only hope.

Penthesilea listened and responded by rousing herself from her mourning, thinking that perhaps by helping the Trojans avenge the death of Hector she could redeem herself of her own crime. Calling for her best warriors, she assembled a corps of twelve women on horseback: Clonie, Evandre, Polemusa, Derinoe, Antandre, Bremusa, Hippotho, Harmotho, Alcibie, Derimacheia, Antibrote, and Thermodosa. The Amazons rode off to find King Priam and announce their intention to be at his service against the Greeks.

King Priam was happy and grateful that Penthesilea had agreed to provide him backup, and he was heart warmed at the sight of the Amazon warriors' arrival. He welcomed Penthesilea joyously and together they enjoyed a great feast which was spread in honor of the queen. When the festivities were over, Penthesilea and her warriors promptly dressed in light armor and made ready to face the formidable enemy. Penthesilea exhibited no fear whatever as she readied herself by donning her helmet and weapons. She carried a bow and arrows, a sword, and the characteristic Amazon double-bladed sword as she led her twelve cavalry into the fray.

The Greeks meanwhile had relaxed their guard slightly, assuming that it would take some time for the Trojan forces to rally after the loss of their irreplaceable leader, Hector. Expecting a bit of a reprieve from the war, Achilles went with Ajax to the Petroklas' grave, where they prayed and offered sacrifices to the gods in memory of their slain comrade.

As Penthesilea advanced boldly with her Amazons, the assembled Greek soldiers all but froze in shock at the sight of the small female force that showed no fear or trepidation, and seemed to come upon them from nowhere. They were taken aback, and perhaps even frightened at the unexpected band of fierce-looking women. Penthesilea immediately fired a small dart into the Greek formation as a sort of warning, and then followed it by charging full force, killing eight Greek captains before they managed to rally their wits. This first attack brought some Amazon fatalities as well, which only served to further incense Penthesilea and cause her to fight all the harder. The battle that followed was a bitter and intense one indeed.

The whoops and screams from the front reached the ears of Achilles and Ajax at the far-off grave. Realizing that they were hearing the sounds of battle, the two quickly armed themselves and went out to assist in holding off the Trojans who were fighting the Greeks on other fronts, in addition to the one where they had squared off against the Amazons. In due time, however, Achilles found himself facing a band of female warriors on horseback with Penthesilea at the front. The queen immediately recognized the hero and his cohort Ajax, both of whom expected her to be taken aback by their presence. Their reputations did nothing to dim her resolve to win, and she recklessly threw a dart in their direction, signaling her willingness to take them on. Achilles deftly deflected the dart using his new shield. The elaborately decorated shield was illustrated with scenes of war which were meant to be infused with a power that would protect the great fighter. Momentarily frustrated, Penthesilea turned to Ajax and fired a dart at him as well. Ajax similarly stood his ground. The entire assembled armies of the Greeks and Trojans stood by watching as this amazing encounter unfolded.

Penthesilea then galloped bravely up to Achilles and introduced herself proudly as Queen of the Amazons and daughter of Ares, the god of war. She brazenly declared that the Greek aggressors were finally about to meet their match in her and her warriors. She conceded that the heroes had been able to escape her darts with their shields, but asserted that they had no hope whatever against her double edged sword and that she would not hesitate to make use of it. Troy would be victorious, she vowed.

Achilles scoffed amusedly at the queen's claim to be descended from the gods. The Greeks, he countered, were the offspring of Zeus – the all powerful father of all the gods. He shouted that Penthesilea would fall, just as Hector had, and that it was she who had no hope of victory over the sons of Zeus. As he let fly these words he simultaneously sent a dart into the air. In seconds, the soft tissue of the queen's breast was pierced, causing a great torrent of blood to paint her lightly clad body crimson. Penthesilea slumped in pain onto her horse's back just as Achilles charged in and stabbed the poor beast at close range, causing it to buckle and fall, taking its injured rider down with it.

Penthesilea lay near her horse, and as the life force left her in a stream of blood, Achilles dismounted his own steed and approached on foot. Bending over her still form he saw that her life was over, and loosened and removed her helmet. (Some versions of this myth hold that Achilles' first dart did not inflict a fatal wound in the queen's breast and that he killed her with a slice

of his sword after she fell from her horse.) At that moment he looked into Penthesilea's still opened eyes, and fell in love. Overcome by her extraordinary beauty and remembering the courage she had exhibited in battle against such a dangerous foe as himself, Achilles was overcome with a deep adoration, mixed with feelings of intense remorse and sadness. Hoisting Penthesilea's lifeless body

carefully into his arms, he held it gently out toward the Greek troops who stood silently watching the scene. Seeing the look of love and compassion on the hero's face, the Greek soldier Thersites jeered at such a show of feelings toward a felled enemy. Hearing this, Achilles fisted his bare hand and struck a blow at Thersites which caused him to fall, never to get up again.

Some writers have claimed the Priam took the body of the queen back to Troy and cremated it, while others say that she was given a burial by Achilles. There is even a theory that not only did Achilles "fall in love", but that he committed acts of necrophilia on the body of Penthesilea before turning it over for its final rest.

Achilles' love for the dead Penthesilea so captured the Greek imagination that it was depicted over and over again in works of art in several media which have been preserved though the ages. However mighty the Amazons may have been, this tale points out what may have been seen as the ultimate truth of male-female relations in the mind of the Greek writers. The woman may fight valiantly as the man, but in the end she can never persevere, and ends up seen primarily as a sexual object to be possessed.

There is an interesting sort of continuation to the story gleaned from later sources which points to the Amazon propensity for revenge and "grudge-holding". According to this version, as Thetis mourned for her son, she had a vision of a sea god who came to her with a message. Achilles may have been dead, the god said, but his immortal ghost ruled a lush island.

When the Amazons got wind of this, it refueled their hatred of the killer of their queen, and they made plans to overtake the mysterious island. When an innocent flotilla happened to pass Themiscrya as it navigated the Thermodon, some Amazons seized the boats and their sailors. Forced into slavery by the Amazons, the sailors were ordered to build a fleet of strong galleys capable of transporting cavalry. Then these vessels were ready, the Amazon army boarded and set wail for the strange island where Achilles was god.

Arriving on the shores of the isle, the women were struck by its unusual beauty and by the thickness of its forests and groves. They noticed a temple rising from a wooded area in the center of the island.

As the Amazons made their way inland on horseback, their animals began became nervous and jittery. The further they pushed on, the more crazed was the horses' behavior until they no longer obeyed their riders' command at all, and began to buck and rear uncontrollably, violently throwing the Amazons to the ground. As the steeds galloped off in a wild dash they trampled the Amazons beneath their hooves and whinnying madly they made straight back to the water. The horses threw themselves over a rocky overhand, dashing themselves to death on the rocks below.

Just then, an intense electric storm blew up, trapping the women and buffeting them helplessly about the island. This storm was so violent and long that when it finally cleared only a handful of Amazons were left alive to make their way back home and tell the tale of the thwarted mission of revenge.

The End of the Amazons...

When the Greeks tried a second time to do away with the Amazons by mounting a serious attack, they did so on Amazon home ground in what has come to be known as the Battle of Thermodon. The Greeks were successful this time, and subdued the Amazons, taking three shiploads of prisoners before setting sail back toward home. Even as defeated captives, the Amazons were not subdued, and as the ships made their way across the Black Sea, they staged an uprising against the ships' crews, getting rid of each and every Greek that manned the ships by tossing them overboard to their deaths.

Once free, the Amazons came into a bit of trouble however, when it became apparent that it may have served them to leave some crewmen alive who had knowledge of the vessels! The women were ignorant of the ships, and though they tried to use the sails and the oars, they were soon hopelessly floundering on a stormy and unforgiving sea. At the mercy of the winds, they drifted into the banks, and after a time they came ashore in Cremni, the land of the Scythians.

The women marched inland, seeking inhabitants, and soon discovered a herd of horses grazing which they immediately mounted and rode whooping into Scythian territory. The hungry Amazons stole cattle and generally caused a ruckus as they galloped about and pillaged the country side. Not surprisingly, the Scythians, assuming they were a band of rowdy young men, came down hard and fast upon them and had soon rounded them up and engaged them in battle. The skirmish was short since the unarmed Amazons were overpowered easily. Only after all the horse-riding marauders were dead did the Scythians realize, to their great surprise, that they were women!

When the Scythian leaders heard about the brave women who had so boldly entered their domain, they demanded that their origins be discovered and that more of such women be brought back and betrothed to the Scythian young men. Scythian soldiers indeed found the remnants of the Amazons and made it clear that they had come in peace. Their proposals of marriage, however, were met with flat refusals. The Scythians were forced to stay in a separate camp, but over time relations between the two groups softened and they were on peaceful terms. A sort of "living together" arrangement was forged between many Scythian/Amazon couples, as the two groups endeavored to learn one another's languages and ways.

In time, the Scythian young men wanted to return to their homeland. Again, they beseeched the Amazons to become their proper wives and join Scythian society. The Amazons refused, stating that they could never get used to the Scythian customs whereby women serve men, after being accustomed to being waited upon by subservient men. The tasks performed by the Scythian women were anathema to the Amazons, and they were loath to give up their animal breeding, archery, hunting, and military skills to stay home quietly and practice the womanly arts. Instead, they suggested to the men that they return home and taking some of their parents' property as an inheritance, return to the Amazons and continue to live in unmarried bliss.

When the young Scythians returned, they were loaded with supplies taken from their families. The Amazons had softened their attitude a bit in the meantime, and suggested that together they all move to a land on the other side of the Tanais. The Amazons were never again to return to Themyscira.

They traveled into the steppes for six days on foot and horseback until they got to the place which is now known as the land of the Sauromatians. The Amazon women lived apart from the men, but in some ways they functioned as husband and wife, regardless. Their offspring, apparently, were the Sauromatians, a tribe whose women were militaristic and continued to hunt and ride. Many of the Sauromatian customs pertaining to women had clear shades of Amazon society, such as the rule that a women could marry only after she had killed a male enemy. Herodotus tells us that many a Sauromate "old maid" lived her life unmated because of this rule. Archeological evidence has been unearthed pointing to the unusually militant behavior of the women Sauromates. Many were buried in full military dress with their weapons at their sides.

Alexander and the Amazon Queen

At the conclusion of the Battle of Issos, in 333 B.C., Alexander the Great was had succeeded in bringing all of Asia Minor under his rule, and the fame of the amazing young conqueror apparently reached all the way to Themiscrya. Diodorus wrote of an incident which occurred after the great battle when Alexander had returned to Hyrcania.

The Queen of the Amazons at the time was Thalestris. As extraordinarily beautiful and striking a woman as can be imagined, Thalestris was also possessed of a rare physical strength and vigor for which she was greatly admired by the Amazons. Thalestris decided to make her way to Hyrcania to meet the legendary young leader and with a full compliment of Amazon soldiers she sailed across the Black and Caspian Seas toward Hyrcania. Leaving most of her troops at the border, she marched to Alexander's camp with three hundred Amazons all decked out in full and impressive military armor.

Alexander received the queen and heard her offer to let him father a child by her. Presumably if the child were to be a girl, Thalestris would take her back to her homeland and raise her. A boy would be raised by his father. Alexander agreed. After all, what better mate could there be for the matchless conqueror than this queen of such amazing beauty and power? The pair agreed to spend a period of thirteen days and nights together, thirteen being a sacred number to the Amazon moon-worshippers. When the time was up Alexander bade the queen farewell. He sent her home to the Thermodon bearing a bounty of wondrous gifts and perhaps pregnant with his offspring.

According to Diodorus' account, however, no child issued from their effort and Thalestris perished in battle only a short time later. Centuries later, Plutarch wrote of the tale, citing many other authors who had meanwhile mentioned it, some of whom reported the story as historical fact, but more having assumed it was fantasy.

LEMNOS

In approximately the year 300 B.C. Appollonius of Rhodes wrote The Argonautic, an epic poem in which we are told about Jason and the Argonauts and their quest for the Golden Fleece. Jason was born the prince of Iolcus, but his evil uncle Pelias had grabbed the throne and sent Jason to live in a secluded cave where he was brought up and tutored by a Centaur. Emerging from the cave as a grown man, Jason returned home to reclaim what was rightfully his.

Meanwhile, however, Hera, the vicious wife of Zeus, had developed her own deep resentment of Pelias, as he refused to honor her as he did the other Olympian gods. Hera hatched a plan to use Jason as her unknowing agent in exacting her revenge on Pelias.

Jason approached his uncle who pretended to receive him warmly, even inviting him to a feast and engaging him in pleasant conversation. Pelias asked Jason his opinion as to what assignment should be given an annoying man one wishes to get rid of. When Jason mentioned

a quest to find the Golden Fleece, Pelias jumped on the idea and sent Jason himself to round up fifty of the fittest men in the land to help him. The fifty became the Argonauts, after their vessel which was dubbed the Argo.

Off they sailed in search of the wondrous fleece. One of the first stops on their odyssey was the island of Lemnos. Some writers have speculated that the inhabitants of Lemnos had some connection to the Amazons, and some even claim that these were actual Amazons that had split off from the Thermodon nation. We can't be sure of either, but what does seem quite certain is that the island was inhabited solely by women and that these women were uncharacteristically violent and headstrong.

Jason and his men had had no former knowledge of Lemnos and when they disembarked on the island as part of their quest, they were quite surprised to find it populated by females alone. In the distance they noticed a large black stone which was atop an altar at the temple of Ares. The Amazons were known to have sacrificed horses to Ares and to hold sacred a black stone, which was also the stone of the goddess Cybele. For these reasons, coupled with the lack of men, it is easy to understand why Jason would assume he'd arrived at an Amazon outpost.

The queen of Lemnos, Hypsipile, led a group of women to meet Jason. Since Jason and his men were attired in full

battle gear, it was not immediately clear that they were of peaceful intent. Jason inquired of Hypsipile as to the unusual status of the island and how it came to pass that there were no men among her people. Hipsipile explained that Lemnos had been subject to an invasion during which every Lemnian man had perished defending the island. The queen even extended an invitation to Jason and his men to remain and take the place of the missing males.

Hypsipile was in fact pulling the wool over Jason's eyes, however. The truth of the matter was that the women of Lemnos had themselves done away with the men. Venus, the goddess of love, had neglected to watch over the Lemnian couples and without her guidance the women had begun to annoy and irritate their husbands. This caused the men to seek more pleasant company in the form of slave girls they obtained in Thrace and brought to the island. The presence of the slave girls and the rejection of the husbands were intolerable to the women and they set about murdering all of the men on the island in response. Even the unmarried men and boys were done away with so that they could not rise up and avenge the deaths of their fathers and friends.

When the women saw Jason and his entourage of Argonauts land on their island they assumed a delegation had been sent to punish them for their deeds. When it was clear that the Argonauts were ignorant of what had taken place, the women lowered their weapons and entreated the men to stay.

Jason and his men were intent on their mission however, and after only a few days (during which it was said they managed to impregnate many of the women) they left the island. The mighty Heracles, who was one of the Argonauts had had enough of Lemnos and entreated Jason to end the visit.

As they sailed away, the Argonauts believed they had narrowly escaped a terrible fate, since they believed they had just encountered the famed and dangerous Amazons.

Later in their journey, the Argonauts passed Themiscrya on the River Thermodon. As they sailed by Zeus sent a north-westerly wind to propel them quickly out of range of the Amazon warriors. Again, Jason and his mighty men breathed a sigh of relief at having avoided a fearful foe.

Much has been written throughout history about the ancient Greek city-state Sparta and its inhabitants. Their disciplined and rigorous lifestyle and their military might spawned the term "Spartan" – an adjective used to describe those who live a life of austerity and stern adherence to the rules of the group.

Another aspect in which Sparta stood out from its rival city Athens was its treatment of women. The female citizens of Sparta enjoyed complete equality with men. They were afforded far more political power than women in other parts of Greece, and even had the right to be landowners in their own names. Spartan women were not considered subservient to their husbands, and in fact could, if they liked, take more than one man at a time in marriage. Like their brothers, they were schooled in fighting and the military arts and expected to be highly disciplined and exhibit physical strength and courage. Speculation as to the origin of these differences and the fact that Spartan women were so independent and strong has included the theory that they were influenced by Amazon lore, or even that they may have been physically descendent from the Amazons.

The worship of Artemis, the goddess of hunting and war, was prevalent all over Greece, but especially so in Sparta where she was considered the patroness of women warriors.

History has not provided an indisputable direct link between the women of Sparta and the Amazons, but the question is certainly food for thought and imagination.

What's in a Name?

The following are the Amazons mentioned in Greek myth.

AIELLO

Aiello's name meant "whirlwind". Armed with the double bladed axe, she fearlessly attacked Heracles in an attempt to prevent him from taking the girdle of Hippolyte. Aiello must have known that it would be futile to fight the invulnerable Heracles, yet she was the first of the Amazon's to come at him in hand to hand combat. Heracles, wearing the lion skin that made his body impenetrable, easily cut down the courageous Aiello. Seeing her fate did not deter eight additional Amazons from trying their might against his in one on one fighting before the Amazon army attacked en force. They too, fell dead at his hand, in this order: Phillipis, Prothoe, Eriobea, Deianeira, Asteria, Marpe, Tecmessa, and Alcippe.

AINIA

Ainia's name meant "swiftness". She fought in the army of Queen Penthesilea against Achilles at Troy.

AINIPPE

Ainippe or "swift mare" fought in effort to avenge the death of Hippolyte.

ALCIBE

Alcibe is mentioned as one of Penthesilea's soldiers at Troy.

ALCIPPE

Alcippe's name meant "powerful mare". She was the last Amazon to engage Heracles in hand to hand fighting. When she fell dead at his hand, the Amazon army attacked Heracles' forces.

ALKAIA

Alkaia, or "the mighty one", was an Amazon general under Andromache.

AMYNOMENE

Amynomene's name meant "blameless defender". She fought with Orithya in Greece during the war against Theseus.

ANAEA

A prominent warrior who ventured out from the Thermodon to conquer neighboring lands, Anaea founded a city which was named for her.

ANDRODEMEIA

"Subduer of Men", Androdemeia fought with Othilia in Greece.

ANDROMACHE

Queen Andromache's name meant "man killer". She led a force of Amazons against Heracles. Several Amazon warriors are mentioned in the ancient literature as having served under her command:

ALCINOE ("MIGHTY WISDOM")

ANTIMACH ("CONFRONTING WARRIOR")

AREXIMACHA

KLEOPTOLEME

KYDOIME

LYCOPIS ("SHE-WOLF")

OKYPOUS

PISTO

SKYLEIA

TEISIPYTE

TELEPYLEIA

THRASO ("CONFIDENCE")

TOXARIS ("THE ARCHER")

TOXIS

TOXOPHILE

Amazons of America

When Christopher Columbus was returning from his first voyage of discovery, he was told by the Indians of Hispaniola of another island, called Mantinino, which was inhabited solely by women. They employed themselves in labour not suited to their sex, using the bow and arrow, hunting, and going to war. Once a year they received Caribs from other islands among them, the men only staying a short time, and on their next annual visit taking away with them the male infants that had been born, the girls remaining with their mothers. These women, besides using bows and arrows, had defensive armour of brass plates. But although Columbus constantly heard rumours of the mysterious island, which often seemed to be in the immediate neighbourhood, yet ever receded, he was not destined to see it or any of its inhabitants. No one, indeed, succeeded in identifying the particular island of which the natives of the Caribbean Sea seemed to give such explicit details.

In 1540 Francesco de Orellana, making his way from far-off Peru to the Atlantic through the Brazils, explored the magnificent river, he and his companions meeting with many difficulties. They were told of warrior women who lived apart from men. when they were approaching the Trombetus River in the neighbourhood of the great, densely wooded island of Tumpinambaranas, they found themselves opposed by warlike natives gathered on the banks, and among them noticed women seemingly acting as leaders of the men, they readily fell into the notion that here they had stumbled upon the renowned Amazons. In this belief they were confirmed by the natives whom they cross-examined, and de Orellana, duly impressed with this wonderful discovery, and some say actuated by a desire to magnify his own exploits, renamed the Marañon River the Amazon, a name subsequently given to a whole vast province.

These rumours of the Amazonian nation were plentiful, but no one ever came across the country, at least no one of sufficient standing to give accurate geographical indications. Father Cristobal de Acuña gave, in his New Discovery of the Great River of the Amazons, considerably more details. "These man-like women," he writes, "have their abodes in the extensive forests and lofty hills, among which that which rises above the rest, and is therefore beaten by the winds for its pride with most violence, so that it is bare and clear of vegetation, is called Yacamiaba. The Amazons are women of great valour, and they have always preserved themselves without the ordinary intercourse with men; and even when these, by agreement, come every year to their land, they receive them with arms in their hands, such as bows and arrows, which they brandish about for a time, until they are satisfied that the Indians come with peaceful intentions. They then drop their arms and go down to the canoes of their guests, where each one chooses a hammock, the nearest at hand, which they take to their own houses, and, hanging them in a place where their owners could recognise them, they receive the Indians as guests for a few days. After this the Indians return to their own country, repeating their visits every year at the same season. The  daughters who are born from this intercourse are preserved and brought up by the Amazons themselves, as they are destined to inherit their valour and the customs of the nation; but it is not so certain what they do with the sons. An Indian who had gone with his father to this country when very young stated that the boys were given to their fathers when they returned the following year. But others--and they appear most probable, as it is most general--say that when the Amazons find that a baby is a male, they kill it. Time will discover the truth; and if these are the Amazons made famous by historians, there are treasures shut up in their territory which would enrich the whole world."

Nuño de Gusman, writing in July 1530 from Omittan to the Emperor Charles of Spain, "I shall go to find the Amazons, which some say dwell in the sea, some in an arm of the sea, and that they are rich and accounted of the people for goodness, and whiter than other women. They use bows and arrows and targets; have many great treasures."

Hernando de Ribera conducting a search party. He came across many natives who reported to him that beyond the Mansion of the Sun-- that is to say, westward of a great lake wherein the sun sank daily to rest--there would be found that much-sought-after country "where women alone dwelt."

Sir Walter Raleigh, in his Discovery of Guiana, says that he spoke to a cacique who had been to the Amazon River and beyond. This chief reported that "the nations of these women are on the south side of the river, in the province of Topago, and their chiefest strength and retreats are in the lands situate on the south side of the entrance, some sixty leagues within the mouth of the same river. The memories of the like women," adds the gallant knight, "very ancient as well in Africa as in Asia, in many histories they are verified to have been in divers ages and provinces, but they which are not far from Guiana do accompany with men but once a year, and for the time of one month, which I gather by their relations to be April. At that time all the kings of the borders assemble and the queens of the Amazons; and after the queens have chosen, the rest cast lots

for their valentines. This one month they feast, dance, and drink of their wines in abundance; and the moon being done, they all depart to their own provinces. If they conceive and be delivered of a son, they return him to the father; if of a daughter, they nourish it and retain it. And as many as have daughters send unto the begetter presents, all being desirous to increase their own sex and kind; but that they cut off the right breast I do not find to be true. It was further told me that if in the wars they took any prisoners that they would accompany with those also at what time soever, but in the end for certain they put them to death; for they are said to be very cruel and bloodthirsty, especially to such as offer to invade their country. These Amazons have likewise great store of these plates of gold, which they recover in exchange chiefly for a kind of green stones, which the Spaniards call piedras hijadas, and we use for spleen stones: and for the disease of the stone we also esteem them. Of these I saw divers in Guiana, and commonly every cacique has one, which their wives for the most part wear, and they esteem them as great jewels."

Of the origin of the "women who live without husbands" a very significant legend appears to have been current along the middle and lower reaches of the Amazon. We are told that in some far-off indeterminate age the women rebelled against their husbands and retired to the hills accompanied by only one old man. They lived by their own industry, quite isolated. All daughters born to this lopsided community were carefully reared, while all boys were killed. Then one luckless male baby, coming into the world deformed and covered with scars, called forth maternal pity. In secrecy the mother lavished all her tenderness and art in the endeavour to cure her child, but without effect until she placed him in a strongly woven bag and squeezed him into a lovely shape. Thereafter he grew apace in seclusion, day by day becoming more charming in form and character. Eventually his retreat was discovered. Then began a long and tender persecution from the women, though the boy remained unmoved. Mother and son consulted together, and to escape his tormentors the youth was thrown into the lake, where he assumed the shape of a fish. Whenever the mother called, the fish swam ashore and was instantly transformed into his beautiful human form, taking food from the hands of his mother. Jealously guarded though the secret was, feminine curiosity soon ferreted it out; and then the other women, imitating the calls, clasped the deceived young man in their arms. It was next the turn of the old man to grow uneasy, for he noticed that he was being neglected. So he set himself to watch, and the spy was driven to fierce anger by the scene of magic

enacted before his eyes. His own calls to the fish were of no avail, so he made strong nets. None was stout enough, however, for always the boy-fish escaped, breaking through the meshes. The old man sat down and thought deeply, and decided upon a plan. Going to each woman of the tribe, he craftily begged them for tresses of their hair. Therewith he made a net so strong and entangling that he promptly caught and killed the fish. After this the women finally abandoned the slayer; but while he was away in his fields, his hut was always put in order by some unknown agency, and his meals prepared for him by unseen hands. So again he hid and set himself to spy. And then he saw a pet parrot fly down, put off her feathers, and swiftly change into a beautiful girl, who at once set about her duties with painstaking industry. To rush forward and fling the feathers into the fire was the work of an instant, then the watcher turned and demanded, "Who are you?" "I am," replied the mysterious squaw, "the only woman who ever loved you. Now you have broken the spell I was under, and I am glad."

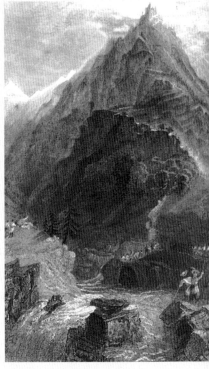

As late as 1743, when de la Condamine was travelling through the country, rumours about the Amazons still persisted, but, like de Acuña, de Ribera, Gili, and many more, this worthy explorer never caught a glimpse of them or the mysterious Manoa. He could only meet people who said they had seen them in some remote, ill-defined region, and who knew others who had years before visited the women and country, which, however, could never be located. When de la Condamine was making his inquiries, it was said that the Amazons had moved off up the Rio Negro, and they continued to retreat before the inquisitive whites into the unmapped forest regions of Guiana. Humboldt, like de la Condamine, was a strong believer in the tales, though his investigations were as little conclusive. Sceptics were equally numerous, and some had made their voices heard even in the days of the conquistadors. There were those ready to insist that the legend grew from the crafty designs of de Orellana, who wished by these devious means to wipe out the memory of his gross treachery to his chief Pizarro, thinking that by marvellous accounts of his own exploits he would wrest applause and rewards from those at home. It is scarcely necessary to attribute wilful intention to mislead on the part of Father Carbajal and other explorers on this head. That women did appear in arms in America as well as in Asia, and for the matter of that in Europe too, there is no reason to doubt. Many instances may be cited.

Juan de lo Cosa reported that when he sailed with Rodrigo de Bastides in 1501 he landed with a party far north of the Orinoco on the site now occupied by Cartagena, and he and his party were boldly attacked by men and women who mingled in the fight, both sexes wielding most dexterously the long dart, or azagay, and bow with poisoned arrows. Hulderick Schnirdel, who travelled in

 company with Spaniards through the country of the River Plate and the Amazon between the years 1534 and 1554, heard much of the fighting Amazons, who were said to live in an island, to have no silver or gold, which they left with their husbands on the mainland--altogether a novel account. Schnirdel went in search of the island, but fruitlessly. He doubted that a nation existed, though he attests that the fighting of women in the ranks with their menkind was common enough. A little later, in 1587, Lopez Vaz recounts the adventures of Lopez de Agira. This de Agira was the rebel and renegade who murdered Don Fernando de Gusman, who had proclaimed himself Emperor of Peru. After the murder, de Agira, accompanied by a few soldiers and natives, started down the Amazon en route for the Atlantic. They met with some opposition, and found it was true that Amazons existed--"that is to say, women who fight in the wars with bows and arrows; but these women fight to aid their husbands, and not by themselves alone without companies of men, as de Orellana reports. There were of these women upon divers parts of the river, who, seeing Spaniards fighting with their husbands, came in to succour them, and showed themselves more valiant than their husbands." But the comparative rarity of the phenomena would be sufficient to stir the imagination of the Spaniards, whose minds, as we have said, were stored with stories of the classic period and tales of the East.

The early Spanish critics accepted the story of the fighting women, as evidence to this effect accumulated, while more or less politely disbelieving the story of Amazon "nations," and their arguments are based on the very fact that women fight side by side with their husbands, and that

such-like warrior women were well known both in ancient and modern history. It must also be remembered that America was still part of the Indies to most of the early explorers, and to them it seemed quite natural that the famous Themysciran nation should have migrated farther afield. It followed that these explorers should find that these warrior women were white, for so the fitness of things demanded, though there is a possible explanation for a light-coloured band of women if we suppose them to have belonged to a semi-religious caste. Then there was another school, holding that this nation of women was the remnant of those who had escaped from Asia through Africa by way of Hesperides or the lost Atlantis. To most of the travellers, as with Father de Acuña, the "Amazons made famous by historians," or, in other words, the Asiatic dames, could not be forgotten, and the stories of fabulous wealth could only contribute to their belief.

The Toltec city of Quiché, capital of Utatlan, Central America, apparently had a population of 3,000,000, and the Spaniards' description of the Royal Palace reads like an account of the Alhambra in its days of glory. Experience taught that it was customary for people threatened with invasion to remove their treasures to as inaccessible retreats as possible, where, also, the womenfolk would be gathered, and these, in default of men, would as occasion demanded take part in the defence of their lares and penates. Villages, too, were often occupied by women, old men, and young children alone for many weeks together, while the men and youths were away on the war-path or some great hunting expedition. Moreover, in this part of the American continent, where moon-worship prevailed, there were certain ceremonies connected with womanhood and child-bearing involving the separation of women from all males, and apparently elaborate dances in the moonlight. Upon these solid enough foundations the Spaniards, by frequently injudicious questioning of the natives, built up a rickety superstructure of many strange fables.

That women did fight on occasion--and this would be particularly true of the hill and forest tribes--we have already seen by various travellers' accounts. That they were occasionally for a length of several moons a tribe, as it were, by themselves, and guardians of tribal treasures, there is no reason to disbelieve. Ample material here for a very robust and circumstantial legend, without either party to the making thereof being, liars of malice aforethought.

An extraordinary fact, which should be mentioned in this place, as it may have some bearing on the subject, is that the Lenâpé tribe of North American Indians were called "Women." They were a branch of the great Algonkin nation, but found themselves down in Delaware, surrounded by the warlike Iroquois. That they could boast of an honourable origin is proved by the fact that the three Delaware sub-tribes had as their totems the tortoise (above all honoured as the servant of the All-Powerful Creator, and on whose back the earth was built up), the wolf, and the turkey. Moreover, Dr. Brinton informs us that Lenâpé means "men of our nation," or "our men." Yet it appears that for a lengthy period this tribe never went to war, and although in later years apparently not held in high esteem, unquestionably filled an important office as a kind of buffer nation of peacemakers. Among most American tribes there existed a Council of Women, composed of the old matrons, whose privilege it was to meet in war-time and discuss matters affecting the tribe. If they advocated peace, it was no disgrace for the "braves" to listen to them and consider the advisability of offering terms to the enemy. It was in some such position as this that the whole tribe of Delaware Algonkins were placed. According to their own statements, the Lenâpés became the peacemaking tribe at the special request of the Iroquois, who saw that the nations were eating each other up. So they approached the Lenâpés with an honourable proposition, and in the presence of the other assembled tribes gave the Delawares the long robe and ear-rings of women, so that they should not bear arms or mingle in strife; the calabash of oil and medicine, to the end that they might become the nurses; the corn pestle and hoe, so that they might cultivate the land; and, in order to emphasise the whole solemnity, bestowed on the chiefs of the "Women" tribe a belt of wampum, the greatest of symbols of peace

and fraternity within their gift, as each division of the strange ceremony was reached. That the Lenâpés fulfilled their mission seems certain, although as time went on the Iroquois began to treat them as a conquered tribe, and used the term "Women" as applied to them with some contumely. This buffer tribe, with its claims to a high mission and its equivocal position and attributes, appears to be unique in American Indian social economy; on the other hand, at all events in the southern part of the continent, there were classes of men in the barbarian nations dressed and treated as women. The whole problem of the "Women" tribe, however, is far from being cleared up. Was it cajoled into its curious place as the result of some dim recollection of a once-powerful women-priest caste? Or was it merely a clever device suggested by pressing needs when it began to be recognised that there must be occasional cessation from the interminable intertribal slaughter? It is a mystery full of suggestion.

It is in this spirit that most of the Amazon stories must be treated. At the same time, we must not omit to quote some weighty opinions pointing to a more direct acceptation. De la Condamine, who was a thoroughgoing believer in the American Amazon nation, argued that its evolution was quite natural and a development for which we might have looked with confidence. He held that the women leading migratory lives, often following their husbands to war, were usually compelled to submit to very harsh domestic conditions. But the very conditions imposed upon them by their mode of life afforded ample opportunities for them to escape from the tyranny by simply detaching themselves from the tribe and forming a community wherein, if they did not exactly gain independence, they would no longer be slaves and beasts of burden. This method of establishing new communities was, he pointed out, going on in every colony where slave-holding was tolerated; the slaves growing tired of ill-treatment escaped to the forests or swamps, setting up their own camps and villages. Robert Southey re-echoed this opinion that "the lot of women is usually dreadful among savages... Had we never heard of the Amazons of antiquity, I should, without hesitation, believe in those of America." To him the terrible hardships of the Indian women's lives demanded some such relief, and he looked upon the existence of such communities as redounding to the credit of humanity, showing that there was hope for its regeneration. A recent writer of deep philosophic tendencies, Mr. E. J. Payne, follows on the same lines. He regards the whole phenomena of Amazonian states as a perfectly legitimate and understandable outcome of the transition from savagery to barbarism, a period when life is peculiarly harsh to womankind. But, as he says, such communities always carry within themselves the seeds of decay, for they cannot extend, cannot indeed exist for long, without the tolerance of man. A day comes when he grows tired of a complacent attitude, and the women then have nothing to do but surrender on his own terms. These are undoubtedly both interesting and plausible theories, which do not really enter into conflict with the opinions that we have ventured to advance on the whole subject.

The Amazone Stone

An outstanding fact connected with the traditions of Amazons in South America is certain greenstones, some form of jade, which the Indians were understood to declare they obtained from "the women who live without husbands." The stones were either roughly wrought in the shape of birds or beasts, or formed into bead-like cylinders two to three inches long, both smooth and in some cases richly carved with curious designs of the intricate, involved kind we associate with Aztec art. Almost always these were pierced longitudinally with round holes, and were worn pendant from the neck as precious talismans.

It is apparent, that these shaped, and mostly graven, greenstones were looked upon as talismans of fertility [for Amazons]. The greenstones were particularly connected with child-bearing. Jade is held in exceptionally high honour in every part of the East, though perhaps most markedly so in China, but the cult for this stone and its congeners extended far beyond the Orient.

the Indians of Brazil declared that the Amazons obtained their treasured amulets from a lake close to Jamunda, a high mountain near the supposed original site of Manoa del Dorado. The Amazons gathered together by night, and, having ceremonially purified themselves, worshipped the moon, invoking her as the Mother of the Greenstones. Then, when the

moon was reflected on the waters, they plunged into the lake, and received the stones from the goddess. Moon-worship was general in the plains of the Amazon. She was the creator of all plants, especially of maize; her subject gods were the increscent and decrescent moons, each of which ruled over minor gods, who were the geni loci of woods, glens, mountains, streams, and lakes, which is the crude form of the belief we have seen existed in Mexico. A curious variant of the story of the capture of the greenstones says that these were alive, swimming about in the lake like fishes, and could not be caught until the Amazons had made personal sacrifice by cutting themselves, when a drop of blood falling over the wriggling green jade acted magically, the stones remaining quiet and

allowing themselves to be caught. At this stage they were said to be soft and plastic; the Amazons took them and with their hands shaped them in the rays of the moon, after which they gradually hardened. These stories, while they connect the greenstones with the heavenly queen, who sent down the vivifying dew and soft light, also seem to bear witness to the difficulty of securing jade or jadeite, which was perhaps but rarely discovered in situ, being mostly derived from erratic blocks and water-borne pebbles.

Guy Cadogan Rothery. The Amazons

The Amazons were proud, capable women who firmly worshipped the Goddess. They bowed to no man for any reason. If history has recorded them as war-like and man-haters, consider that men of strictly patriarchal cultures persecuted and killed them for their beliefs, then wrote the histories. The Amazons refused to submit to the loss of their freedom and rights, therefore they were considered to be dangerous and unnatural. Their extinction was brought about by the Greeks and other patriarchal societies because of the Amazon's fierce defense of the matriarchy and the rights of women.

D.J.Conway

"Their costume is usually a short tunic girt up for action, frequently open at one side in order to display the woman's figure. Long narrow trousers, long coat/tunic, and soft, long boots, panther skin capes and armor. The effort is always, not to show them to be foreigner's who wear a fantastic garb, but to indicate plainly that they are women warring with men."

florence mary bennett-Religious /cults Associated with the Amazons

Russian Female Warrior

Nikolay Nemytov in his book "Battle fighters" cites interesting analysis of the ancient images of battling Amazons. He derived from them that the ancient female warriors were very skillful but fought just like women – they developed the special female combative strategy fitting women's particular features.

She grabed hold Dobrynya by yellow curles,
Turned him down out from his good horse,
And dropped Dobrynya in a deep bag...

...Our story about epic heroes would be partial if we don't mention the legendary glorious female warriors named "Polenitsa". That was the name of a girl or a woman who engaged in a field duel with male hero warriors. On a level with male warriors they were sitting on the honor feast of the Grand Duke Vladimir "Red Sun". Epic heroes engaged with female warriors in duels and Polenitsas weren't inferior to men in strength and adroitness and sometimes even outdid them like legendary Nastas'ya Nikulishna.

The best description of an ancient Russian female warrior is done in the epic poem "Ilya Muromets and his daughter". Polenitsa is very tall and she has a totem – coat of arms. "On her right arm a "nightingale" is sitting, on the left hand – a lark. A combat helmet covers her head with a face-like visor and fur under-helmet. Neither Dobrynya nor Alesha take a risk to fight with her. The only great Ilya – tsar-warrior engaged with her in a combat".

They don't beat each other mercilessly,
They don't knock down each other from horses,
They don't hit or wound each other either,
Nothing is bleed -
When they have broken the spears
And notched the swords,
They just engaged in the fisticuffs
This Polenitsa was quite daring
And besides, maliciously quick-witted
She was taught to fight by one hand…
She toppled Ilya on the ground by a treacherous move.

The information about Polenitsas is very scanty and it's difficult to say if they had their own knight Order. Unlike epic heroes who were sole-worshipers they used bird totems which was a common sign for them. Bird totems make Polenitsas to be related to the Amazons who battled Greeks and Greeks left a lot of information about those ancient female warriors.

Let's pay attention to numerous images of battles between Greeks and Amazons and may be we will manage to discover something new. Analyzing the images we can derive some battling techniques the Amazons used. First of all, we must note that women hand-to-hand combat is different from men's one just because a male body is not adapted to carry embryos and to give birth; consequently their body are very different. So do battling tactics. Female battle is a trick, adroitness and nothing from strength confrontation is impossible. It looks like a sweetheart has been caught and is already in your hand but it was not to be! She just allowed to come near, pretending amenable, weak. But don't be surprised if the ground falls onto you and you feel nauseous by slight tough of tender fingers. Those contemporary martial art teachers who make artificial creatures from girls who are able to physically resist men just pervert them forcing to go against their nature. In fact, the Amazons were horrible element, however they didn't forgot about their main function to give birth and continue their race. Having killed a certain number of enemies a female warrior had rights to select a husband equal with her in battle trade, even from enemy camps. That's why female combat style should be different from the men's one. For a reason it was said that a Polenitsa was "maliciously quick-witted".

Let's examine the three images of the Amazons in battle (see the vase drawings page 116). Pay attention to male warriors attacking female opponents. Perhaps, in a moment the exhausted Amazons will fall down under mortal Greeks' attacks. This imagination is a spark of the female style, which misleads male attackers. We will consider separately each combat episode.

Fist episode (left vase, upper pair). The woman is stepping back turning her body by the right side to the opponent, threatening from above with the sword leaving her liver vulnerable. The male warrior aims directly there, his sword points from below. He encounters two problems though: it's more difficult to hit the opponent's body disposed sideways and besides, in order to strike the receded opponent he should either stretch ahead or strike with a step. The Amazon enticingly exposed herself; he can protect himself from her desperate strike by the shield, but her side is so close and the man makes a direct thrust. Possible Amazon's actions: she shifts her center of gravity to the leg moved aside. She makes a move toward his shot with the 1800 turn; the right armored arm makes a sliding block against the opponent's arm. Thus the woman's chest turns out to be next to the right shoulder of the man and

her weapon appears just next to his open belly - his shield is on the left and his right arm with the sword is stretched ahead in a vain attempt to touch the enemy.

Second episode (right vase, upper pair). The Amazon's position seems to be critical but, once again, it's just at first glance. She disposes in a deep sitting and her opponent attacks her by the spear from above pouncing on her by all his men's strengths. Indeed, the Amazon is like a string in such a stand. She turns her body around turning her shield toward the spear; she shifts the left leg ahead and at the same time stands up crushing the unprotected enemy's head and chest by the shield whereas her sword (or the javelin) strikes the Greek's open belly. The struck down warrior is sliding along the Amazon's shield by inertia of his own stroke and he is thrown to the left from her. The Amazon might see an alluring temptation to chop off the supporting leg of the Greek by her leg as they do that in karate-do, then the enemy's body would fall on her. But a hitch happened in a battle may cost the life.

Third episode (left vase, lower pair). The female warrior is also in a deep sitting while the male warrior exposed himself in fever of the battle and might be easily caught. The Amazon is supposed to shift from one leg to another exposing the shield under a stroke and appears on the right from the opponent, just next to his open belly. She also has an option to clip his vein inside of his thigh.

Thus the impression of the overwhelming Greek superiority would turn out to be their crash. It's important to note that a defending warrior is in such stands during fractions of a second transferring from one combative move to another. So, the artist made the excellent snapshots of these quickly changing poses. The Greek artist killed two birds by one stone: he represented the triumph of his fellow warriors and, at the same time, he truly drew the Amazon's perfect combat moves. But possibly the artist was a talent slave from a tribe allied to the Amazons and knew what he was drawing?

From the book "Battle fighters" by Nikolay Nemytov

"The Greek writers seemed to have no doubt that women could destroy whole populations of adult males, and there was no effective defense against them."

Barbara Walker,The Woman's Encyclopedia of Myths and Secrets

The Greeks reported that the Amazons were great tamers of such wild animals as lion, panthers, deer, bulls, goats, rams, eagles and falcons.

Pausanias, Description of Greece, 8.22.5

Pausanias also saw and described the religious sanctuary built by the Greeks of Stymphalos and dedicated to the goddess Artemis. He reported that the temple had carvings of the Stymphalian birds up near its roof. Standing behind the temple, he saw marble statues of maidens with the legs of birds.

...reported by Herodotus: Amazons tattooed themselves. Amazon women covered themselves with geometric and animal motifs.

Amazons are the first to mount horses and to use iron.

(Lysias, Funeral Oration 4)

ANDROMEDA

Andromeda's name meant "ruler of men". She fought under the leadership of Andromache.

ANTANDRE

Antandre meant "going before men". She fought under Queen Penthesilea at Troy.

ANTIANARA

Queen Antianara succeeded Penthesilea after the latter was killed at Troy.

ANTIANARA

Theseus was one of the Amazon fighters who engaged Theseus in hand to hand combat during the Athens war. Antianara explained why the Amazons crippled the men they kept in their midst as slaves. We might have assumed that this was done in order to ensure that the men would not escape or rise against their keepers. However, Antianeira said that lame men were the most proficient lovers. This is interesting in that it points up the possibility that the Amazons not asexual accept when procreation was needed and were indeed not adverse to sexual relations with men simply for pleasure.

ANTIMACHOS

Antimachos is mentioned as one of the fighters of the Athens war.

ANTIOPE

An Amazon of striking beauty, Antiope was the wife of Theseus, King of Athens. According to one version of her story, Theseus was with Heracles when he came to Themyscira to obtain the girdle of Hippolyte. He abducted Antiope and carted her back to Athens where he legally wed her or held her captive, depending on which version is read. Another story tells us that Theseus did not come to the Thermodon with Heracles and that Heracles brought Antiope to Athens and presented her to the king. Either way, the marriage made Antiope the only Amazon known to have been married. Regardless of the circumstances of her union with Theseus, she apparently fell in love with him. She bore him a son whom they called Hippolytus, after Antiope's sister, Hippolyte. When the Amazons came to Athens to wage war against the Greeks in revenge for her kidnapping, Antiope fought on the side of her husband, defending Athens against her own people. She was killed by Molpadia, and Amazon warrior who felled her by stabbing her to death with a spear. Another version of the story of Antiope's death holds that Theseus planned to take a second wife, and seized with powerful jealousy she raided the wedding along with a band of Amazons and was killed by Heracles in the ensuing skirmish.

ARETO

Areto "the Unspeakable" led a band of Amazons in a successful raid against Heracles and his men after the murder of Hippolyte.

ARISTOMACHE

Aristomache, the "best of warriors", took part in the war in Athens against Mounichos.

ASTERIA

Asteria, whose name meant "of the sky", was the sixth Amazon to die when she engaged Heracles in single combat when he came to the Thermodon on his quest for the girdle of Hippolyte.

BREMUSA

When Penthesilea marched to Troy she was accompanied by twelve Amazon soldiers, of whom Bremusa, or "raging woman" was one.

ANTIOPE

Antiope defended her Amazon sisters using her archery skills in the Athens war.

ANTRIBROTE

Under Penthesilea, twelve notable Amazon warriors liberated Troy temporarily. Antribote was one of the twelve

CLEITE

Queen Cleite, whose name meant "invoked", sailed for Troy to join Penthesilea. She and the warriors aboard her vessel never reached their destination. They were blown off course by a storm and eventually landed in Italy where they founded a city which bore the name of the queen.

CLYEMNE

Clyemne of "famous might" fought hand to hand against Theseus and Phaleros in the Athens war.

DEIANEIRA

Deianira's name meant "she strings up the spoils". She was the fifth Amazon warrior to face Heracles in hand to hand combat. In another story of Deianeira (perhaps another warrior of the same name) she falls in love with Heracles and bears him several children. When he eventually tires of her, she commits suicide.

CELANEO

Celaneo, along with her constant cohorts Euryhe and Phoebe was an Amazon warrior who was expert at the use of the spear. She and her companions were killed by Heracles.

DEINOMACHE

An Amazon soldier whose name meant "terrible warrior", Deinomache fought in the war in Athens.

DERIMACHEIA

Derimacheia was one of Penthesilea's twelve companions when she went to fight at Troy.

DERINOE

One of Penthesilea's twelve, Derinoe kill Lagonus in face to face fighting.

DORIS

Doris' name meant "bountiful". She wielded her spear with cunning during the war in Athens.

ERIOBEA

One of Hippolyte's faithful soldiers, Eriobea was the fourth Amazon to face Heracles and lose her life in hand to hand fighting.

EUMACHE

Eumache's name meant "good fighter". The resourceful Eumache fought the Greeks using stones when her quiver of arrows was empty.

EURYBE

Eurybe's name meant "grand strength". Part of an inseparable threesome of warriors, Eurybe fought alongside Phoebe and Celaneo. All three were killed by Heracles' sword when his impenetrable lion skin garment repelled their arrows.

HARMONTHOE

One of Penthesilea's twelve companions, Harmonthoe fought at Troy. Her name meant "sharp as nails".

HIPPO

One of the greatest of the Amazon queens, Hippo's name meant "horse". Under Hippo the Amazons conquered many lands, pushing into Asia Minor and Syria. The Amazons under Hippo founded city after city, among them Ephesus, Smyrna, Cyrene, and Myrina. Ephesus became the site of the great shrine of Artemis. The city became a destination for frequent pilgrimages by Amazons and rites and rituals around the worship of Artemis were performed there.

HIPPOLYTE

Hippolyte was another variation of the name meaning "horse", (in this case "stampeding mare", a sacred and important symbol for the Amazons. The beautiful Hippolyte was a prominent and forceful queen. It was her golden

girdle, which had been given to her by father, the god of war, Ares that was the object of the ninth labor of Heracles. His quest for the girdle brought him and his band of fighters to the shores of the Thermodon, setting off a chain of events that eventually led to the Amazon war in Athens.

A second Amazon bearing the name Hippolyte was the sister of Queen Penthesilea. In a tragic hunting accident, Penthesilea accidentally killed Hippolyte, which led to her expedition to Troy, and her own death.

HIPPOTHOE

This name meant "imperious horse" and belonged to one of the Amazon companions to Penthesilea in Troy.

HIPSIPILE

Hypsipyle's name meant "of the high gate". One of Hippolyte's faithful warriors, she fought against Heracles' captains.

IPHITO

Another warrior of Hippolyte's, Iphito also fought against Heracles' captains.

LYSIPPE

Lysippe's name meant "she who frees the horses". She was one of the most prominent Amazon queens and her warriors expanded the women's empire deep into Asia Minor. Lysippe's soldiers were fierce and proud, using their brass bows and powerful horses to ensure victory after victory. Lysippe was responsible for the building and strengthening of the Amazon city Themiscrya and for establishing many of the customs and rules of the Amazon lifestyle. Under her rule the Amazons solidified their hold on the Thermodon area and introduced the use of cavalry to her warriors and to the world. She raised numerous

shrines to the goddess Artemis and gave thanks to the goddess for each military victory the Amazons attained.

Lysippe's story had a tragic twist. She gave birth to a handsome son whose name was Tanais. In Amazon society males were not to take part in war, and Tanais' desire to do so coupled with his refusal to look for love outside of Themiscrya angered the goddess of love, Aphrodite. As punishment, Aphrodite caused Tanais to fall in love with his mother. Since of course such a love could never be consummated, Tanais fell into despair and eventually drowned himself in the Thermodon. Lysippe was inconsolable and threw herself into her queenly and military roles with a vengeance, using her energies to strengthen the Amazon nation. Lysippe eventually met her death in battle.

MARPE

Marpe was the seventh Amazon warrior to challenge Heracles and to lose her life in hand to hand combat with the invincible man.

MARSEPIA

Queen Marsepia, whose name means "the snatcher", was a strong military leader under whom the Amazons raided Thrace and Syria. Later she marched along with Hippo and together they founded the cities Ephesus and Cyrene, making their way as far as the Aegean Sea. After returning home to the Thermodon, news of an uprising in Asia in one of the conquered areas

reached Marsepia and she traveled back there with her warriors in order to solidify their hold on the area. She was killed in attack on this mission.

MOLPADIA

Molpadia's name meant "death song". She was one of Queen Orithia's faithful warriors. According to one legend, Molpadia fought in Athens to rescue the Amazon queen from Theseus, and she was able to make her way into the king's castle. When she discovered that her fellow Amazon had fallen in love with her captor/husband and did not wish to be rescued, Molpadia drew her sword and killed the former queen. Theseus then put Molpadia to death.

MYRINE

Myrine was queen of the Libyan Amazons, hundreds of years before the Thermodon tribe settled Themiscrya. Her name meant "swiftly bounding" and she was a strong and charismatic queen. Myrine led her warriors into nearby Atlantis where her army of over thirty thousand strong soundly defeated the defenders. After the victory, Myrine managed to establish a truce with the Atlantans and protected them against their other enemies, the Gorgons.

Myrine later died in battle at Thrace, and an "Amazon hill" was built over her grave.

OMPHALE

Queen Omphale was said to have ruled the southern Libyan Amazons. According to myth, when Heracles was put under a spell he killed his wife and children. To atone for these sins he was sold to Omphale as a slave and he was forced to serve the queen wearing women's apparel and performing menial and traditionally female duties such as spinning and weaving. When he

displeased her, Omphale beat him with her golden sandal. In the end, Omphale grew tired of her slave and sold him back to the Greeks.

ORITHYA

When Marpesia died in battle, her daughter Orithya became the Amazon queen. She made a pact with the Scythians and along with a force led by the son of the Scythian king the Amazons avenged the Asian barbarians that had killed Marpesia.

OTRERA

The name Otrera was a title given to distinguished Amazon leaders. Its origin was in the name of the ancestral goddess of the Amazons. Otrera and the god Ares parented the nation of the Amazons. Also according to myth, Otrera was the name of the goddess mother of Queens Hippolyta, Antiope, and Lysippe.

PANTARISTE

After the battle that took place following Heracles' ninth labor, the Greek captains fled back to their vessels. Pantariste and a band of Amazons made chase after them, viciously killing those that attacked her.

When Tiamides tried to make his way back to his homeland to alert Theseus about the coming Amazon attack on Greek soil, Pantariste thwarted his plan by murdering him.

PENTHESILEA

Perhaps the greatest and best known of the Amazon warriors, Penthesilea was the daughter of Ares and Orithya. Penthesilea was as skilled in military arts as she was exceptionally beautiful. The brave queen was also known for

compassion and wisdom. Tragedy fell on Penthesilea's life when she and was out hunting and the queen's weapon accidentally slayed her sister, Hippolyte.

Penthesilea's was inconsolable, and decided to leave the Thermodon, using the Trojan War as her destination. She selected twelve warriors to accompany her and they helped to liberate Troy. However, Heracles overtook it and after success at killing many other Greek warriors, Penthesilea found herself in single combat with him. She tried to hold her own, but of course was ultimately vulnerable to the invincible hero. When Heracles beheld her lovely face after her death, he fell posthumously in love with her. The name Penthesilea meant "causes men to mourn".

PHILLIPIS

Phillipis, whose name meant "woman who loves horses", was the second Amazon to engage Heracles in hand to hand combat when he came to Themiscrya for his ninth labor.

PHOEBE

Phoebe was part of a trio of warriors along with Celaneo and Eurybe. They met their death at the hand of Heracles during the ninth labor.

POLEMUSA

Polemusa was one of the twelve warriors accompanying Penthesilea when she fought in the Trojan War.

PROTHOE

The third Amazon warrior to lose her life in hand to hand combat with Heracles, Prothoe's name meant "first in might".

PRYGOMACHE

An Amazon fighter whose name meant "fiery warrior", Pyrgomache was mentioned as having taken part in the Athens war.

TECMESSA

The eight Amazon to die fighting Heracles during the ninth labor, her name meant "judge".

THALESTRIS

During Alexander the Great's Asian campaign around 350 BC, he is said to have had a short relationship with the Amazon queen Thalestris. She visited the young conqueror in his camp and offered to bear him a child. After spending thirteen nights and days of love with Alexander, Thalestris returned to her people. She may have been pregnant, but went to her death in battle soon after.

THERMODOSA

This Amazon warrior was chosen as one of the twelve companions of Queen Penthesilea at Troy.

VALASCA

Queen of the Amazons for a short time, Valasca was a particularly cruel ruler. Under her queendom males living among the Amazons all had their right eyes and thumbs removed to ensure their inability to do battle against the women warriors. When Valasca died, the Amazon community heaved a collective sigh of relief and resumed its normal ways.

XANTHIPPE

A fighter in the war at Athens, Xanthippe's name meant "yellow mare".

Conclusion

Even when divested of adventitious adornments, there remains a remarkable body of evidence as to the widely prevailing belief in the existence of countries, districts, or islands populated solely by women. it is clear that the Greek myth is not sufficient to account for all the stories, though it is, of course, indisputable that these legends have largely colored most of the tales that have reached us.

It is possible to divide roughly the legends and traditions into three main classes. We have:

(1) Women living apart in colonies, but having occasional communications with the outside world on a peaceful footing.

(2) Women banded together as a fighting organisation.

(3) Nations ruled over by queens, and mainly, or to a considerable extent, governed by women.

Varied as are the stories which we have reviewed in the foregoing pages, it will be seen that they all fall into one or other of these divisions.

It must be admitted that as society emerges from savagedom into barbarism on the road towards civilisation, the burthens of the respective sexes are readjusted, and not without considerable friction and discomfort. Sometimes the whole tribe will move from winter to summer quarters, but often enough it is the men alone, with the growing lads, who go off on active work, leaving the homes to the safe-keeping of the women, with a sprinkling of old men and small boys. ...No doubt in certain stages of society the whole tribe moves, and the women, especially if of a hardy mountain or forest stock, would naturally share all forms of activity with the men within the measure of their strength, and the more skilful of them would be found in the fighting ranks with the male warriors. Thus it comes about that historians and travellers tell us now of unisex organisations, and then of women in Asia, Europe, Africa, and America – using the bow and arrow, the sling and the lance, aiding and abetting their husbands and brothers in martial exploits. As we have in effect already observed, the

juste milieu is never a strong point in feminine nature, and so fighting woman becomes in very deed an "unholy terror," something particularly abhorrent to those who are fresh from casting off the fetters of barbarism. The ratio between fighting men and women would constantly vary under the influence of seasons or tribal evolution, and so tend to further accentuate error of judgment, giving rise to robust myths.

... Religious ceremonies in which only one sex could take part, and which we find among barbarians and even the highly civilised Greeks and Romans, would cause the sexes to divide up temporarily into unisex tribes in the more primitive states. The Amazons of Asia, we are told, were worshippers of Artemis (Astarte), who had her great mysteries only to be witnessed by women, as well as ceremonies in which both sexes mingled in secret and openly.

Reviewing the whole subject, it seems clear that it is to religious influences that we must trace the existence of many, and probably the most startling, traditions concerning bands of women

warriors and women societies. It reveals one of the most sombre sides of the human intellect. We have to go to the dark Caucasus to find the origin of the Greeks' Amazons. Here it was that Prometheus, who had stolen fire from heaven and placed divine truths at the service of mankind, was fettered to the rocks, exposed to the torture of the eagle until that bird, the emblem of priestcraft, was slain by Hercules. This was merely a symbolical presentation of what was actually taking place. For here too, as Strabo reveals, the Albanians had a sanctuary dedicated to the moon-god, a temple wherein men were sacrificed by a spear-thrust, the priests watching the fall and gush of blood for purposes of divination, after which the body was removed to a stated spot so that the people might take an active share in the sacrifice by trampling on the scapegoat and purifying themselves thereby. Farther to the north-east, at Phanagoria, near the Palus Mæotis, he also tells us, was a shrine to Venus Apatura, the Deceitful, who, having secured the aid of Hercules,

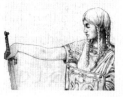

allured her admirers one by one into a cave, where they were killed by the sturdy sons of Jupiter and Alcmena.

The Babylonian trinity consisted of Anu, the Creator; Sin, the sun god; and Ishtar, the moon goddess, who wore the crescent. As the planet was credited with influence on fertility generally, we have one reason for certain specialised sacrificial ceremonies connected with the worship of that goddess in her many manifestations, from the grim Ishtar to the more gentle, though often cruel, Venus.

Some hint of this we have in relation to the Amazons of the Caucasus, who, according to Strabo, spent two months of each spring on a neighbouring mountain which formed the boundary between their own territory and that of the Gargarenses, who also ascended the mountain, so that, in obedience to ancient custom, they might perform common sacrifices. They met "in secret and in darkness," as might be expected from worshippers of Astarte. Evidence of other forms of self-sacrifice seem to be referred to in the legends of the American Amazons, e.g. (1) those who, in order to obtain the fertility talismans, had to wound their own bodies and offer  their blood; (2) the whole Amazon tribe disappearing in a hole in the earth, led by an armadillo. Again, we have the tale of the infant placed in a bag and squeezed into a new and beautiful shape. As de Gubernatis has shown, the sack has two symbolical meanings: it is the night, or the clouds hiding the sun--therefore death; and it also denotes the act of devouring, another form of death. But night and death, though a conflict with the sun and light, are merely means to renewed life. The American Amazon sacrifices her boy so that he may have a beautiful rebirth, and, as we know, the saintly youth goes through a second form of sacrifice, being thrown into the lake and metamorphosed into a fish, that other symbol of life-giving power, and as such is worshipped by the women and finally again sacrificed. This sacrifice, it will be remembered, was effected by means of entanglement in a net woven from the hair of women. Now, in many places the worship of the moon goddess entailed abandonment of the female body within the dark temples to all strangers who might come, or in lieu thereof the milder offering of their tresses.

We are told in the Maha Bharata that Shantanu, descendant of Chandra, the great moon god of Northern India, married the incarnated Ganges. This beneficent river goddess had assumed human shape as a penance, probably in order to obtain greater power, and on her earthly pilgrimage she had met seven minor gods, who told her a most piteous tale. By an unlucky chance, these mystic seven had come between a holy hermit and his sacrifice, and he, being a man with enormous accumulated power as the result of long-continued acts of austerity, had, with the usual irascibility of the self-righteous, cursed them with the terrible doom: "Be born among men." So Ganges, taking pity on them, married Shantanu, and the seven sons of the royal and divine pair were the seven gods. As each was born, his earthly destiny having thus been fulfilled, she threw him into the mighty stream, whence he straightway entered heaven.

Here, it would seem, is a clear allusion to offers of human sacrifices to the fertilising goddess-river. It corresponds with what we know of the great Nile Sed ceremonials of the Egyptian flood time. Greatly modified, we find it again in the marriage of the Doge of Venice with the Adriatic, the Doge casting into the waves a symbolical ring that he might gain dominion over them; and yet again in the blessing of the waters, whether it be by priests in the Mediterranean or by czars on the Neva; or again by the offerings freely given by fishermen, which may take the form of the silver coin placed by Yorkshire boatmen in the corks of their nets, or the casting of the Adonis gardens into the waves by Sicilians and others. All these are sacrifices meant to repay the rivers (or the sea) for their gifts of food and prosperity to the people, sacrifices which in the case of the Ganges were afterwards softened into the custom of throwing the dead, or their ashes, into the sacred waters, so that they might be born again into a higher sphere, and in that of the Nile by the substitution of flowers for the maidens.

Herodotus has a curious story about the Libyan Auseans, who dwelt on the shores of Lake Titonis. Their maidens once a year held a feast in honour of Minerva. This we may take to be Neith or Nit, – that is, Night, – whom the Egyptians regarded as one of

the trio of primitive gods, as the Mother, Nature, or in some sense the First Principle, and whom they depicted as a nude black female, arched over, resting on finger-tips and toes, bespangled with stars to represent the vault of heaven. At these celebrations it was the custom for the girls "to draw up in two bodies and to fight with staves and clubs." The loveliest maiden was clad in armour, of Greek design in the days of the chronicler, who wonders, but cannot guess, what manner of defensive gear they had worn before they came into contact with the Hellenes. Those of the girls who fell in the fight were declared to be "false maidens." Herodotus goes on to say that the Auseans held that Minerva (Neith) was the daughter of Neptune and Lake Titonis, and was adopted by Jupiter. The whole of this is suggestive of religious celebrations carrying out the idea of conflict between two elements or powers, good and evil, with the underlying notion of the benefits to be derived from sacrifice. The Ausean genesis of Neith is a tale of opposing influences, some life phenomena observed as the outcome of the blending of salt and fresh water under the action of the sun. It was appropriate enough that the ceremonies connected with the birth of the grim primitive Neith should be an affair of the armed guard of maidens and associated with strife between light and darkness, the triumph of the true devotees and the slaying of the false.

In early stages of civilisation the king is usually a god-king, and later a priest-king. It was a high office, but, as we have seen, one often fraught with awful consequences; for the divine ruler passed to the other world self-immolated, or by the assistance of his priestly attendants, who often were women. Thus we see the Behr king on the White Nile surrounded by a female guard, strangled when on his death-bed. This form of "happy dispatch" for honoured persons was widely prevalent. It still survives in a degraded form among the "Fish-Skinned" Tatars of the Amur. These degenerate nomads, who live on fish and dress in fish skins, habitually strangle their old folk with certain suggestive ritual. Drums are beaten, and all persons leave the camp except the victim and two near relatives, who act as executioners, or rather sacrificers. The grim work is carried out in the tent while the drums are being beaten outside. That women guards took part in such ceremonial death-

scenes has been shown, and their semi-sacerdotal office is evident in many ways. Snelgrave reports that in his day the King of Dahomey, though not secluded, yet kept aloof from his people and even his courtiers. His chiefs and others during audiences, having prostrated themselves and kissed the ground, whispered whatever they wished to reach the royal cars into those of an old woman, who went to the king, transmitted the message, and then returned with the answer.

Which shows another stage in the intervention of the privileged councillor between the sacred person and the supplicant. Then, as we know, the petty King of Abeokuta, also on the west coast of Africa, was guarded by women, while in the same region the King of Yoruba formerly possessed a female guard, and the executioner "wives" of the King of Wydah were 5000 in number.

Turning in another direction, we find the same thing presenting itself at Pataliputra in the Punjab, and we hear of Indian rajahs going out hunting surrounded by armed female warriors, corresponding in this particular with the King of Dahomey and his picked Elephant Huntresses. In Bantam it appears to have been the custom for the women royal guards to elect from among their own sons a new king in default of a direct heir. All this we may compare to Megasthenes' account, who says that the women guards at Pataliputra were at liberty to kill the king if found drunk, the executioner marrying the successor.

Throughout all this we may note differences of detail, but the mission of these women as a buffer class between the claimant to superhuman attributes and his people is clear enough. How illuminating, therefore, to find this phenomenon of organising a special guard of women repeating itself in Eastern China in the fifth and sixth decades of the nineteenth century, as though spontaneously evolved from the exigencies of the case. When those misnamed "Princes of Peace," the Tae-pings, inaugurated a vast religious movement, they declared that they were expecting a sacred leader. To them appeared that "Celestial Virtue," Tien-wang, and, claiming both divinity in his

own person as second son of God and dominion over the world as regent of the Celestial King, it seemed to follow naturally that he should be protected by a bodyguard of women warriors. And although the religious movement quickly assumed a political phase, the fanatical aspect only increased as the Celestial King and his female guard swept through the land, carrying fire and sword in every direction in the name of peace and goodwill.

It is remarkable that the ancients in writing of the African Amazons, and American Indian traditions, describe the warrior women as a "white" race. It has been argued from this that both the African and American Amazons must have been emigrants from Europe or Asia. But assuming that there was foundation for the reports, the fact would be capable of quite another interpretation. It would point, indeed, to an exclusive class. As Sir Richard Burton rightly says, though in a different connection: "Rank makes some difference in colour; the higher it is the fairer the skin. . . . Even amongst the negroes of Central Africa we find the chief lighter-tinted than his subjects." To the black or copper-coloured a slight lessening in shade means "white." Tradition, therefore, seems to indicate, at all events in the earlier stages, the existence of an exclusive caste of warrior women both in Africa and America, and with some associated idea of self-sacrifice.

They were, like the Lenâpé "Woman" tribe of North America, and the mutilated beings of Central and South Africa, as well as of Asia Minor in ancient times, somewhat in the position of scapegoats.

Captain John Adams, writing about the Congo (in 1823), says: "One of the conditions by which a female is admitted into the order of priesthood is leading a life of celibacy and renouncing the pleasures of the world." This renunciation was certainly the prevalent idea as regards the Dahomeyan Amazons in the early days, and perhaps also, so far as regards the queen, in the regions of the White Nile. At least one of the Portuguese missionaries declares that the queen of the Abyssinian Amazons was looked up to by her neighbours as a goddess, and the same was said of the mysterious foundress of that equally mysterious second great will-o'-the-wisp golden city of the continent, Dobayba, about which Vasca Nuñez de Balboa and his successors on the Isthmus of Darien heard so much and dared many perils in vain to seek. Certain legends said that Dobayba was a mighty female who lived at the beginning of time, mother of the god who created the sun, moon, and all things--in fact, the supreme Nature goddess. Others asserted that she was a powerful Indian princess who had held sway among the mountains, built a beautiful city, enriched with gold, and gained widespread renown for her wisdom and military prowess. After her death she was regarded as a divinity and worshipped in a golden temple. Traditions were persistent of a rich concealed temple, where neighbouring caciques and their subjects made pilgrimage, carrying offerings of gold and slaves to be sacrificed. Neglect of these rites brought drought, most dreaded of Nature's punishments. Farther south we hear much the same tale of the Brazilian warrior women (who were "whiter than other women") in Nuño de Gusman's letter to the Emperor Charles V.

Two matters may be touched upon lightly: the association of the Amazons with sun and moon worship and with cannibalism.

Strabo is our authority for the sanctuary to the moon god in the Caucasus and the shrine to Venus Apatura, while we know the Greeks all declared the Amazons worshipped Artemis (Astarte) and carried crescent-shaped shields. In Africa such records as we have connect the women warriors with the sun god, as evidenced by their use of snake skins, alligator and tortoise emblems, and their alliance with Horus; but Ptolemy refers to the Moon Mountain in Central Africa, apparently in the regions where the Abyssinian and White Nile Amazons were placed. In America we find the association with moon-worship both through the legends and the greenstone fertility amulets. In the mountains of the upper reaches of the Amazon River, however, we find great peaks crowned by temples bearing symbols both of the sun and moon, and other mountains called the Mansion of the Sun, the Seat of the Sun, and so on.

... In Greek tradition the Amazons not only fought and overcame the man-eating gryphons, but, according to some, helped Hercules in his struggles with the Hydra, and farther back assisted Dionysus against the giants. As to the early African Amazons, we also see them waging war against the savage black races, who, on the testimony of even late Arabic authors, we know, "ate men"; and this warfare was carried on, Pigafetta tells us, by the Congo Amazons and the giant anthropophagists down to the end of the sixteenth century.

It is curious to find that where rumours of fighting Amazons are most persistent we have abundant proof of primitive savagery lingering on. The fabulous Isle of the East, inhabited by women, where human sacrifices prevailed, was called El-Wak-Wak because "Wak-wak" was the only word uttered by the ceremonial victims. The Western African women, in their endeavours to reach Egypt, had to pass through a land peopled by cannibal tribes bearing the repeat names Nem-Nems, Gnem-Gnems, the Niam-Niams of to-day, who call their neighbours the Akka Tikki-Tikki. In the Amazon valley and the Andes such duplication is common as regards topographical names--for instance, the Huar-huari and Pina-pina rivers, Lake Titikaka; the mountain Sara-sara; Chapi-chapi village; and there is also the Inje-inje tribe, who are extremely retiring forest folk, still in the stone age of development, and are supposed to use only the one word "inje" doubled, with different inflexions to express all their wants and feelings, in this resembling the tree-grown puellæ Wakwakiensis. This repetition in all kinds of ways is a favourite form of emphasis with primitive people, just as it is with small children.

In passing, we may note the fact that in the three great centres of Amazonian traditions – in Asia, Africa, and America – though we have mention of mountains and forests, the real seats of activity are on extensive alluvial plains. Such situations have always been cradles of new nations and of social revolutions, for

it is in these rich granaries that peoples mingle, man multiplies, where interests clash, giving rise to upheavals and abnormalities, until a new order of affairs has been evolved.

That there was some justification for the legends there can be no reasonable doubt. The very diversity met with in regard to them is strongly in favour of some solid foundation having existed; because, if we consider them critically, they answer to some need of humanity. If we take into account the tendency, on the one hand, to exaggerate, and on the other the frailty of mankind in the matter of giving and receiving evidence, we have much still left. We know that the Greeks loved the declamatory form; the Orientals revel in the superlative. We have seen the pitfalls that beset the inquiring explorers in America, and we have a similar note of warning from West Africa, where Father Bouché says: "Native interpreters aim less at being very accurate than at not displeasing the white man. They do not fail to flatter him by giving translations which they know he desires, or rather which they are aware will fall in with his views."

Even apart from what we may be permitted to call these amenities of the "traitrous translators'" art mistakes may arise innocently enough from sheer confusion of tongues, a blundering all too easy in matters both great and small, as daily experience sufficiently demonstrates. Take as an instance a little incident that came under the writer's own observation. A very small boy was in the habit of calling a particularly favoured lady of his acquaintance his "clean friend," to her immense delight but to the scandalised bewilderment of the child's parents. Then it was discovered that the youngster had been translating Italian into English through the medium of French. "Propria" became "propre," and, of course, "propre" meant "clean," therefore "il mia propria amica" ("mine own particular friend") became his "clean friend." Assuredly perfectly logical, and not without a certain poetical symbolism of speech all the

more pleasing for its very spontaneous unconscious cerebration, yet which, under different circumstances, might have proved grotesquely misleading. We are all – savages, barbarians, and civilised – little children in this transmutation of thought into concrete phrase, with the help of all too unstable words and the evasive flux of grammatical rules. Yet admitting all this, and allowing it to have due weight in its application to our particular study, we may conclude that the legends should be credited to a large extent

Even thus stripped of much of the marvellous, the problem is intensely interesting. While teaching us the fundamental unity of nature, manifested not less in the tendency to fall into error and distort half-truths until they degenerate so far as to seemingly sanction ghastly practices, than in its aspirations to higher things, it happily points to the immense strides accomplished in the march of progress. Onrushing waves necessarily involve the disconcerting phenomena of reflux eddies, which seem to tell of the elusive nature of hope, so that we are often cast down as we reflect on present conditions and contrast them with the near past, mellowed as such views are into a haunting beauty by the glamour of blurring sentiment. Nevertheless, if our retrospective glance is sufficiently comprehensive, the evidence of secured progress is unmistakable, and so we are heartened to look forward to a bright future that assuredly will not be ours, but to which humanity is heir, and whose advent we may all in some measure contribute to hasten.

Guy Cadogan Rothery. The Amazons